THE TOUCHSTONE PRESS
P. O. Box 81
Beaverton, Oregon 97005

Southwest Washington Cascades

INDIAN HEAVEN
Back Country

Trails • Lakes and Indian Lore

by MEL HANSEN

ACKNOWLEDGEMENTS

This book is the result of beneficial input from many people. I am personally indebted to all of them and particularly wish to acknowledge those who were especially helpful.

Historical Information
Jim Attwell
Robert and Myrtle Overbaugh
Frank (Ernie) Childs
Spencer Frey

**General Information
and Trail Logs**
U.S. Forest Service Staff
Gifford Pinchot National Forest

**Wild Flower Information
and Photographs**
Elizabeth Horn

Photography
Hugh Ackroyd
Bill Cogdall
Ray Filloon
Tom Worcester

Copy Editing
Lillian Mosher
Frank Murray
Jean Baldwin

Indian Heaven Map
Richard Hammond

Trail Sketches
Don Oliver

Line Drawings
Bear-Cougar-Big Foot-Trout
Don Oliver

**Constructive Criticism
and Encouragement**
Bill and Joyce Cogdall
Gene and Renee Sellman
Cal and Helen Storey
Don and Patty Murray
Wiley and Bev Bucher
Velma Runger
Vern Galaway

Hiking Companions
Bill Cogdall
Jim Hansen
Don Hedges
Cal and Helen Storey
John and Jan Rian — Kirsten,
Anne Marie, Gene and Renee
Sellman — Greg, Mike, Lyn and
Eula Hansen — Nancy, Patty,
Bill and Lucille Belleville

Riding Companions
Spencer and Erma Frey
Bill Cogdall
Glenna Hite
Jackie Petrin
Tom Worcester

CONTENTS

INTRODUCTION

Eighty-five miles from Portland, Oregon, or Vancouver, Washington, lies a mystical land used and loved by the Indians longer than can be remembered. This area was known to the Indians as "Sahalee-Tyee" (Great Spirit). Because of the history of Indian use, it is known today as Indian Heaven.

The Indian Heaven back country is located astraddle the crest of the Cascade Mountains in Skamania County, Washington, approximately twenty miles north-northeast of the town of Stevenson, lying in the Mt. Adams Ranger District near the southeast corner of the Gifford Pinchot National Forest. The Pacific Crest National Scenic Trail system traverses the area from south to north.

The main part of Indian Heaven contains a concentration of some 150 lakes and meadows lying at about 5,000 feet elevation. The arrangement of these lakes and tarns interspersed with the meadows, the scattered true fir, noble fir and mountain hemlock and the gardens of wild flowers, make the area a place of breath-taking beauty.

Several impressive mountain peaks are present and range in height from 5,050 feet to just under 6,000 feet. From their summits and slopes a spectacular panorama of the timbered Cascade Range with its snow-capped giants unfolds on all sides as far as can be seen.

At least three well-defined craters are located in the area. Lemei Rock, the highest point in Indian Heaven, is one. A second lies on the eastern edge with Wapiki Lake, a deep blue jewel, in its bowl. The third, East Crater, is a distinct, well-formed cinder cone rising 600 feet above the meadows and forming a perfect crater 375 feet deep. Of these, East Crater has been designated by the U.S. Forest Service as a potential geological area. The round appearance and depth of Lake Sahalee Tyee suggests that it, too, may have been formed as a result of past volcanic activity.

Indian Heaven has no roads within its boundaries. Forest Service roads exist on all sides with access trails leading into it. These Forest Service roads are accessible from the Portland-Vancouver population centers via Highway 14 on the Washington side or Interstate 80N on the Oregon side to the Washington towns of Carson, Cook and Bingen. Either the Bridge of the Gods at Cascade Locks or the Hood River Bridge may be used to cross from Oregon to Washington if the chosen route is 80N.

From Carson, a county road runs north up the Wind River Valley intersecting forest roads providing access from the west and south. From Cook, a county road leads north seven miles to Willard where it intersects with Forest Service roads providing access from the south and east. From Bingen, State Highway 141 connects Trout Lake with the main Highway 14. The Randle-Trout Lake Road N123 intercepts State Highway 12 and furnishes access from the north and northeast. From Woodland, Washington, County Road 503 leads to Cougar where it joins Forest Service roads providing access from the west.

The best time to visit Indian Heaven is the fall of the year when the snow has melted and the mosquitoes are scarce. During this time the high meadows change from various green hues to a myriad of yellows, browns and reds as the sedges, grasses and low huckleberry brush prepare for the dormant season. In the crisp fall air, the blue sky, dark green forest and brilliant foliage provide a kaleidoscope of color.

Detailed directions to specific trail heads are included in *Trail Descriptions*. All Indian Heaven trails are restricted to backpacking and the use of saddle stock.

PART 1:

History and Background of Indian Heaven

HISTORY

Until the early 1900's the Indian Heaven back country was a famous summer meeting place for northwest Indian tribes who came to pick huckleberries (olallie), race their horses, play games, make baskets, hunt, make jerky, tan hides and fish in the many lakes. The local Indians (Siwash) were joined by tribes from as far away as Montana, but most came from The Dalles, Yakima and Warm Springs. They would bring with them their wives, children, dogs, horses, robes, furs, weapons and every bit of their property that they could carry along. A favorite camping spot was the Indian Race Track, a huge meadow located at the base of Red Mountain and one-half mile west of the Pacific Crest National Scenic Trail No. 2000. An Indian named Alec Silas reported seeing thousands of Indians on the Crest Trail during the summers of 1903 through 1905. An early newspaper clipping described a 1911 visit to the race track by Pioneer George Beetsch and family:

☐ *"George Beetsch and family returned on Saturday from the huckleberry fields near Trout Lake. They had a fine trip. One of the places visited was the old Indian race track where 600 Indians are now camped. The squaws picking and drying the huckleberries, the bucks gambling or racing horses many of which are fine animals. It is expected that about 1500 Indians will be in this district by the first of next week."*

The race track was known to Indians far and wide. One tribe would bring their best horse (cooley-kuitan) to race another tribe's best horse. The Indians would line up on both sides of the track to watch the race. Bets were wagered, and at a signal the two fast horses were off, racing from the east end of the track to the west, where they would be slowed by running up the hillside. Some reports have it that on occasion they would turn and race back to their starting point. The Indians would stake everything on the speed of the pony: robes, goods, and horses. With the fever of gambling upon them, some would not hesitate to stake and lose the clothing off their backs or even their faithful squaws. The last horse race was held in 1928, with the stakes being the loser's horse.

If you were to visit the Indian Race Track today, you would see the groove worn by the ponies' hooves. It is still plainly visible being ten feet wide, over 2,000 feet long and depressed into the earth several inches. Over the years trees encroached onto the westerly end of the

10

track. Some pioneer descendants were upset about this condition and stated, "If the Forest Service won't remove the trees from the track, we are going to do it." During the summer of 1976, the descendants carried out their threat.

In addition to horse racing, the Indians enjoyed playing games. One of their favorites was a game called "chall chall" involving sticks, beaver teeth or small bones. The players would sit opposite each other, usually three on a side; sometimes they sat cross-legged and other times they knelt facing each other. Each side had a number of small sticks stuck in the ground for keeping score. When all were ready and the stakes or prizes were put up, a song was struck up with the pounding of sticks on a piece of wood, adding to the excitement and the confusion. One side would start passing the two small beaver teeth or bones from one fist to another with great speed, nimbly crossing and recrossing arms. The wrists, fists and fingers of the players were muffled with bits of fur or leather in order to deceive their opponents. The quickness of the motions and the muffling of the fists made it almost impossible for the opponents to guess which hand held the beaver teeth, which was the main point of the game.

Tanning a hide

Indian woman drying huckleberries. Below: The baskets were made from split cedar roots. Bear grass (also called squaw grass) was dyed and used for the design. These early photos of Ray Filloon were remarkable in that most Indians were reluctant to have their picture taken. Some believed that the picture would cause their lungs to shrivel.

While the player was doing all the maneuvering, his opponent eagerly watched his motions trying to discover which fist contained the beaver tooth. The opponent pointed with lightning speed at the fist he thought the tooth was in, the player at the same time extending his arm and opening the fist. If it was empty, the player drew his arm back and continued, while the guesser forfeited one of his ten score sticks.

If the guesser hit upon the fist that contained the beaver tooth, the player gave the guesser one of his ten sticks and ceased playing while the guesser tried his hand at juggling the tooth from fist to fist. When one side won all ten sticks of its opponent, the game was over. Before another game started the winner collected his winnings, which could be everything he owned. Men who lost everything, sometimes sold themselves into slavery. They were well treated while able to work, but when sick or old, they were often neglected or even turned out to die.

The Indians played other games such as "Omintook." This game is mentioned in historical writings but is not described.

Some old timers believe these summer celebrations were first held in the vicinity of Sheep Lakes but were later moved to the race track when encroaching trees prevented the huckleberries from ripening. There is some historical evidence to support this belief. Captain George McClellan (a Union Army General during the Civil War) and his men were instructed by the War Department to search for a pass through the Cascade Mountains for a railroad route to the Pacific. In 1853, McClellan reported a large Indian encampment at Sheep Lakes. In his exploring McClellan buried a cannon near one of the huckleberry fields. Treasure hunters are still looking for the old cannon 124 years later. In 1936 the Forest Service reported, "Halfway up the south ridge of Berry Mountain is a grave dated 1853. A rock bears the name of Smith. It is thought the grave is for one of McClellan's men."

In the days before the Merwin, Yale and Swift Dam impoundments, salmon came up the Lewis River to spawn. It is said that the Indians would make side trips from the Indian Heaven berry fields to catch the salmon and make pemmican. Their gathering spot was the falls at the confluence of Chickoon Creek and the Lewis River.

It is quite possible the Indians' use of Indian Heaven was temporarily stopped when Mt. St. Helens erupted in 1842. A dense layer of ash was deposited throughout the area as far away as The Dalles. A second interruption probably occurred during the 1855-1856 Indian Wars when the Yakimas, Klickitats and many of the Cascade Indians attacked the North Columbia River portage settlements in the area then known as the Rapids or Cascades.

Commencing in the late 1800's, the white man grazed sheep in the Indian Heaven meadows. The practice was stopped in 1944 because the Forest Service believed the fragile meadows (with their short growing season) could not withstand the abuse.

To this very day the Indians visit the vicinity of Indian Heaven. They arrive each year at the "Sawtooth" huckleberry fields. They do not come on foot or ponies, but in 20th Century mechanical vehicles to where a portion of these berry fields (area east of Forest Service Road N123) is reserved for their exclusive use in accordance with an old agreement with the U.S. Forest Service. Here visitors may observe tent and tepee encampments.

BIG FOOT TERRITORY

Skamania County, Washington, is known to many as "Big Foot Territory" because of the number of purported sightings and encounters with the giant, hairy creatures that have been reported throughout the area. Because of the many reports, the American Yeti Expedition, co-sponsored by *National Wildlife* and Robert Morgan of Miami, Florida, chose Skamania County to concentrate its search efforts. The Board of Skamania County Commissioners passed an ordinance* assessing a fine of $10,000 and up to five years imprisonment for killing a Big Foot.

Because of my curiosity about the English meaning of Indian words and names, especially the Indian named lakes in Indian Heaven, I found some interesting information about Big Foot that predates reported stories of the last sixty years. A Chinook-English dictionary gives the English translation of Cultus Lake as **Bad Lake**. I questioned why the Indians considered Cultus Lake to be bad. Was the water unfit to drink? Was the lake devoid of fish? Was the area avoided by the Indians and, if so, why?

Mrs. Robert (Myrtle) Overbaugh of White Salmon, Washington, informed me that she had an 84-year-old Klickitat Indian friend named Bessie Quaempts who might be able to provide the answer. Her friend was reluctant to be interviewed by white strangers, however, and Mrs. Overbaugh suggested she conduct the interview. I provided Mrs. Overbaugh with a few simple questions and here are the results of the interview:

Question: Did the Indians ever mention a "Big Foot" or "Sasquatch"?

14

Answer: "Yes, Big Foot is called 'Sehlatiks'."

Question: Did the Indians ever see Sehlatiks?
Answer: "Yes, many times."

Question: Did the Indians camp and fish at Cultus Lake?
Answer: "No, many Sehlatiks people there. Indians afraid of Sehlatiks people."

The Yakima Indians, who also visited Indian Heaven, considered the Sehlatiks to be wild outcasts of the mountain tribes — evil spirits to be avoided. They believed the Sehlatiks were also located in other areas such as Mt. St. Helens and Mt. Adams.

It is interesting to note that many of the Indians' descriptions of Big Foot are identical to those of the white men — gigantic in size, two legged, covered with hair, walks upright, smells bad, screams and whistles.

The Skamania County Big Foot came to the attention of the American public in the year 1924 when five gold prospectors came roaring into Kelso, Washington, with a hair-raising story about their encounter with a Big Foot family in the vicinity of Mt. St. Helens.

Two of the men were hiking up a trail when they saw a huge, hair-covered monster looking at them from behind a tree. Both men fired their guns and claimed to have hit the ape-like creature, but it ran off into the woods.

Two days later, Fred Beck, one of the prospectors, went hunting for deer as they were running short of camp meat. He followed a canyon and when reaching the top ran into a Big Foot. It started to run, and he shot it several times in the back. It stumbled and fell off the canyon rim into a raging creek several hundred feet below.

Beck ran back to camp, gathered the men, and searched the creek area where the creature had fallen. The raging torrent had carried the Big Foot downstream.

As it was getting late in the day, the men decided to return to camp and resume the search the following morning.

In the middle of the night they were awakened by ear-piercing shrieks and the crunching of huge boulders on the roof of their log cabin. They were afraid to venture outside, so punched holes in the chinking between the logs so they could fire their guns. Because of the darkness they could not see their targets, so they fired blindly to scare them away. The attack lasted for some time, but finally the creatures went away.

At first light the prospectors dared peek out the cabin door to make sure that none of the creatures were still around. Then they quickly grabbed their gear and raced down the trail to their car.

Upon reaching town they told their story to the sheriff and to newspaper reporters. Two search parties were quickly organized and headed back to the mountains. The searchers could not believe what they saw. Dozens of huge foot prints up to 17 inches in length, blood-stained rocks, wisps of coarse dark hair and the wrecked cabin. One of the huge boulders remained lodged in the cabin roof, and it took two men to roll it off the roof to the ground. How strong must one of these goliaths be to hurl a boulder of this size? The search

party combed the area, but never caught sight of another Big Foot.

Meanwhile, the story was receiving wide coverage in the newspapers, and reader reaction was mixed from "belief" to "hog wash."

Ever since this incident the canyon has been called "Ape Canyon," not to be confused with the lava "Ape Caves" near Cougar, Washington.

As time went on all five prospectors deserted the Kelso area. Their friends say they left because they objected to being called crazy liars.

Many believers say there would be far more reportings but for concern about being laughed at. What would you do if you actually saw Big Foot? Would you report it or remain quiet because of fear of ridicule?

If Big Foot exists, why hasn't he been shot by one of the hundreds of hunters in the mountains? A British Columbia highway construction worker named William Roe gives a possible clue. He had climbed Mica Mountain in search of a lost gold mine near Tete Jaune Cache when he saw Sasquatch walking out of a clump of bushes. He described the creature as being about six feet tall, almost three feet wide, and probably weighing near three hundred pounds. It was covered from head to foot with dark brown hair. As it came closer he saw by the breasts that it was a female. Her head was higher in back than in front, her nose broad and flat, the eyes small. In a short time she caught his scent and stared directly at him. Her face expressed fear as her eyes widened, her lips parted and she walked away hurriedly, looking over her shoulder to see if she were being followed.

Roe brought his rifle into shooting position and put her in his sights. He could not pull the trigger because, "I felt now that it was a human being and I knew I would never forgive myself if I killed it."

Only one believable photo of Big Foot has ever been taken. The late Roger Patterson of Yakima captured him on film in the fall of 1967. One of the best prints taken from the 16mm color film show Big Foot walking, arms in movement, the upper portion of the body and face looking back at Patterson. The picture received national publicity through newspapers, magazines, radio, television and movies. John Napier, then Director of the Department of Primate Biology for the Smithsonian Institution obviously believed the pictures to be authentic. He volunteered to be the narrator for films to be produced professionally based on Patterson's original pictures.

In early December of 1976, the writer traveled the Gifford Peak Way

Trail with Spencer Frey of Trout Lake, Washington. The trail was the last one that needed to be documented for inclusion in this book and weather and time were becoming a matter of concern. In order to hurry things along, Spence brought two of his finest pack horses. The sun was shining, but the ground was frozen and the lakes were icing around the edges.

We stopped for lunch in a pretty meadow alongside Darlene Lake. Spence turned the horses loose to graze while we proceeded to enjoy some cold meat sandwiches, pickles and homemade cookies.

As if on signal, the two horses made a complete turnabout and stood facing the trees surrounding the meadow to the south. They continued to stand, frozen in this position as though hypnotized.

Spence said quietly, "Something's out there!"

In another moment there was a crackling of brush, and the horses commenced to fidget. I asked Spence if I could borrow his handgun and go take a look. (He carries the gun in the event a horse should break a leg, etc.) I eased into the woods, moved around for awhile, but never saw a thing.

We packed up and moved across the trail to find the lakes on the north side. We found a beauty and were admiring it when, all of a sudden, a roaring growl came from across the lake about 300 feet away. The horses half-reared and I exclaimed, "Wow, what was that?" Spence replied, "Mel, I don't know." We listened for a long time but never heard another sound.

Spence and I discussed the incident for most of the way down the trail. He was with the Forest Service for many years and, after retirement, packed people into the wilderness for hunting and recreation. He commented, "I've heard bears bawl, cougars scream and elk bugle, but never a sound like that." We talked about the big grey wolf as a possibility. The big grey wolf lived in this country in the 1800's, but is thought to be extinct.

About the time we returned to the car I hesitatingly mentioned the subject of "Big Foot." Spence confessed to having thought about it, but was reluctant to mention it to me.

I cannot honestly say whether I believe in Big Foot. I do, however, know one thing for sure. When I walk past Cultus Lake this summer, or the Darlene Lakes, I am going to keep my eyes and ears open. I will probably breathe a little easier when I get well beyond those areas. Who knows? Maybe I will see Big Foot.

18

FISH

In the late 1800's a self-appointed game protector from Husum, Washington, took it upon himself to pack fish into some of the Indian Heaven Lakes for stocking. His name was Guy Mordicai Jones, an Irishman who had earlier immigrated from England. He was an ingenious man, building his own hatchery and stocking it with German brown trout, also known as Montana black spotted trout. He continued to plant the lakes for many years. Robert Overbaugh, born at White Salmon in 1893, said he saw fishermen bringing out trout from the lakes when he was a kid. Whether the fish planted by Jones were the first fish in these lakes or whether some were stocked before is a matter of debate. Some say the Indians were catching trout before Jones' time while others say this is untrue.

A hatchery was built at Goose Lake in 1929 and Frank E. (Ernie) Childs, former Recreation Technician with the Mt. Adams District of Gifford Pinchot National Forest, packed many of these fish into the high lakes. These fish were also brown trout. Unfortunately, this hatchery was washed out by a flood in 1933.

For some reason, the Forest Service poisoned some of the lakes to get rid of the brown trout. They then joined with the Washington State Game Department and planted rainbow trout from a hatchery on the Columbia. The rainbows did not do as well as the browns.

Subsequently, the Washington State Game Department took over the planting of the lakes and air-dropped brook trout and cutthroat trout exclusively.

In recent years the writer has talked to a number of fishermen who claim to have caught brown trout and rainbow trout as well as the state-planted brook and cutthroat trout. This matter was discussed with Ernie Childs and he agreed it could be true. He recalls that the water level of the lakes was extremely high at the time they were poisoned to eliminate the brown trout, and that some of the brown trout probably survived.

Guy Mordicai Jones left no plant records, so it is not known which lakes he stocked. Many of the smaller lakes are deep enough to withstand winter freeze-out, and he may have planted some of these along with the larger lakes. Early Indian and sheepherder trails led to some of these lakes which are now off the existing trails. The subject certainly excites the curious, and the writer intends to compass his way into some of these lakes, both named and unnamed, to determine whether they hold fish.

The Washington State Game Department records show the following plants:

Cultus Lake	Cutthroat
Deep Lake	Brook — Cutthroat
Placid Lake	Brook — Cutthroat
Elk Lake	Brook — Cutthroat
Deer Lake	Brook — Cutthroat
Clear Lake	Brook — Cutthroat
Bear Lake	Brook — Cutthroat
Eunice Lake	Cutthroat
Heather Lake	Cutthroat
Dee Lake	Cutthroat
Thomas Lake	Brook — Cutthroat
Wood Lake	Eastern Brook
Sehalee-Tyee Lake . . .	Brook — Cutthroat
Blue Lake	Brook — Cutthroat
Wapiki Lake	Cutthroat

A fisherman should not be surprised if he catches rainbow and brown trout from these lakes as well as brown trout from other lakes in Indian Heaven.

WILDLIFE

Indian Heaven provides food and cover for many species of birds. These residents include stellars jay, Canada jay (camp robber), bald eagle, osprey, duck, goose, raven, ruffed grouse, blue grouse, and many other small species.

The big game inhabitants are elk, deer and bear. Other mammals include cougar, wildcat, raccoon, mink, otter, beaver, porcupine and hoary marmot. The grey wolf was present in the 1800's and early 1900's but is now thought to be extinct. (An old Indian Heaven map

20

shows a "Lake Le-Loo." The word Le-Loo is Chinook for the "Big Grey Wolf.")

Some animals, under certain conditions or circumstances, could pose a threat to personal safety.

DEER

One is not likely to meet a semi-tame deer in Indian Heaven back country, but should one appear, it is unsafe to feed it by hand. Their hooves are sharp and if they become impatient, they can lash out with a hoof, causing serious injury.

NOCTURNAL ANIMALS

Nocturnal animals wandering around during daylight hours should be given a wide berth because they may have contracted rabies. Coyotes and foxes, for example, would be suspect if they appear to have lost their natural fear of man or are unstable on their feet.

THE BLACK BEAR

The Indian Heaven back country contains a sizable population of black bears, but unlike Mt. Rainier and Yellowstone National parks' bears, Indian Heaven bears rarely appear when man is near. These bears have not yet been introduced to people food and are quite content with their natural diet of grass, berries, grasshoppers, fruits, nuts, roots, mice, ground squirrels, etc.

Although there have been a number of documented unprovoked attacks in Alaska, British Columbia and elsewhere, black bears generally stay clear of people and mind their own business. It seems reasonable to believe that these rare unprovoked attacks were made by the one in ten thousand "Loco Renegade." The odds are also high that you will never meet him. As opposed to the "unprovoked" attack, however, the "provoked" attack can be a matter of concern. Mama bear is very protective of her babies. A hiker must stay on the alert to never come between a mama bear and her cubs. A good idea is to make a little noise now and then so that a bear is not surprised, and shouting periodically is a good idea when on a trail showing bear signs. Some people prefer to blow a whistle; however, a whistle could be mistaken for a hoary marmot, and a bear could come running toward the whistle instead of away from it.

Black bears have been clocked at running speeds of nearly thirty miles per hour, so one is not able to outrun a bear charge. They are great tree climbers and scrambling up a tree to get away is useless. Some old timers claim they have quietly talked a bear out of a charge, but this procedure is not recommended and would have no effect if a mama bear's attack was already under way. The best precaution is to let the mama bear know a person is around so she has time to move her cubs away from the area.

Unlike the black bear, the grizzly bear of the Canadian Rockies is another story. He is unpredictable, and has been known to charge without provocation. The accounts of women in menstrual periods being attacked and carried away in their sleeping bags are true. No such incident involving the black bear has ever been reported.

Although black bears are present throughout the entire Indian Heaven back country, a particularly heavy concentration of bear signs has been observed in the Rock Lake to Blue Lake portion of Trail No. 111, and on the Indian Race Track Trail No. 171 from Road N605 to the Race Track. In some portions of these areas the huckleberry-filled droppings were located at 100 to 200 foot intervals in the center of the trail — so much so that one might wonder if the bears weren't saying, "Hey, you, this is our country — keep out. We're letting you know how we feel by doing what we're doing right in the middle of your trails."

Do not take a dog into bear country. Usually bears will run from a dog, but not a mama bear with cubs. (The following will illustrate what could happen. "Dog chases bear! Mama bear chases dog! Dog runs back to whom?")

When bears become a camp nuisance, it is because people have allowed them to become so. To leave out garbage or leftover food is an invitation for repeated visits by Mr. Bear. The night sounds of a

BLACK BEAR

22

bear prowling camp can be unnerving, particularly when miles from civilization. It is not likely to happen if all Indian Heaven visitors will leave a clean camp and pack out leftover food or garbage that cannot be burned.

Campers in national parks reportedly have had to cut their trips short because bears had stolen their food. A simple way to solve this problem is to put all food in a plastic bag, tie a rope onto it and hoist the loose end over a tree limb at least 12 feet off the ground. Pull the bag up under the limb and secure the loose end to the tree trunk. Be sure that the limb is insufficient to support the weight of the tree climbing bear and that the food is far enough away from the tree trunk so that the bear cannot reach it.

Keep in mind that camp bears are not after people — they are after food. **Never** sleep with food in a tent or next to your body.

COUGAR

Many persons who have spent years in the wilderness have never seen a cougar. This is why he is called such names as "mystery cat" or "ghost." Stories of attacks on man are rare, although killings have been documented in British Columbia. Other known attacks were made by old or emaciated animals incapable of serious harm. Cougars will normally flee the approach of man.

If deer are available, a cougar will kill one every week to ten days. Cougars also kill calf elk and smaller prey. They cover their kills with litter and return to feed again. The cougar generally selects the infirm

23

and diseased animals, thereby helping to maintain healthier game herds.

The adult females and males live alone and fend for themselves. The female raises a litter of two or three kittens for about two years with no assistance from other adults. Cougar kittens are able to kill small prey when only a few weeks old.

Females are strongly territorial, defending their five- to fifteen-square-mile areas against other females. Males wander over larger areas, often overlapping in the territories of two or three females.

Cougars establish areas, space themselves and communicate by depositing scented urine as they move along, by scraping ground cover clear — a visual "mark" which may be a warning — and probably by vocalizing. These signs allow cougars to locate one another for breeding, to avoid others when the possibility of a serious confrontation exists, or to avoid an over-crowded hunting area.

When a female enters mating condition, her odor changes and she attracts males who follow the scent trail to find her. The caterwauling, likened to a woman's scream, also signals mating condition. The mated pair remain together for about one week and then separate. In about three months the litter is born, usually in the late spring and summer. Though cougars are capable of breeding throughout the year, the tendency to seasonality found in the Northwest prevents the loss of young to extreme cold. It also affords them more food.

When the litter reaches a certain stage of maturity, normal predatory behavior of the mother instinctively changes so that her young may experience and practice their inborn skills to kill. They must learn what to hunt, and acquire confidence, for as youngsters they are naturally fearful of any larger animal. The mother does not kill prey she catches, but instead mauls it or simply releases it in the presence of her young. When a herd of sheep is encountered, for example, a rancher may lose as many as two dozen lambs in one night, with only a few being fed upon. Fortunately for both the cougar and the rancher, these occurrences are rare. Most mother cougars live far from ranches or do not dare come this close to civilization.

The Washington State Game Department carefully monitors cougar hunting to prevent a decline. Their biological evidence suggests the State's cougar population is on the increase. Valid estimates in 1974 put it at 1,500. The game department informed this writer that cougars are present in the Indian Heaven back country, and I have observed their tracks on Trail No. 111 just north of Lake Sahalee-Tyee.

WILD FLOWERS

Wild flower displays occur everywhere in Indian Heaven. You will see them along the roadside approaches to the trail heads and on up the trails to the spectacular displays in the high meadows. Most of the flower illustrations appearing in this book were chosen because of their use by the Indians for food, dyes and medicinal purposes. The photos and the information contained herein was furnished by Elizabeth L. Horn, author of two best-selling books called *Wild Flowers I* and *Wild Flowers III*.

AVALANCHE LILY

The avalanche lily bulb was readily eaten by the Indians who boiled it or dried it for storage. They also used the leaves and ate them raw. The fresh seed pods were boiled and taste much like string beans.

Wherever the snow has melted, this lily carpets mountain meadows and forests.

ASTER FLEABANE

The name fleabane comes from the old practice of hanging these flowers in a room to rid it of fleas. This colorful plant can be found at timberline and in alpine areas.

Avalanche Lily

Aster Fleabane

CREEK GOLDENROD

The yellow flowers of some species of goldenrod were used to make a yellow dye, lending color to Indian crafts and clothing. The Indians also boiled the leaves to make a preparation to put on cuts and flesh wounds.

The creek goldenrod may be found along stream banks and other moist areas below timberline.

FEW-FRUITED DESERT PARSLEY

The thick, fleshy roots of the few-fruited desert parsley were used by the Indians for food, either roasted or raw.

The journals of Lewis and Clark tell of purchasing these roots as food for the group.

This little parsley abounds on open pumice soil and dry slopes near timberline. Although the flowering stalk extends only four or five inches above the ground, the fleshy tap root may be more than one foot long.

SALAL

The dark blue berries of the salal were highly prized by the Indians.

Creek Goldenrod

Few-Fruited Desert Parsley

Salal

These utilitarian fruits were gathered and made into syrup or dried and ground into flour and stored as flat cakes. The early settlers used them for pies and jams. Salal berries are preceded by flowers which bloom from mid-May through mid-July, depending on elevation.

MOUNTAIN SORREL

Climbers and backpackers find mountain sorrel leaves pleasantly sour and a refreshing change in their diet of freeze-dried food. The leaves can be eaten as salad greens and are rich in Vitamin C.

Mountain sorrel grows in moist ground, usually in rock scree or crevices above timberline.

SNOWBUSH

Many snowbush species contain saponin, which gives the flowers and fruits soap-like qualities. Both the Indians and pioneers used the flowers as a soap substitute.

This evergreen shrub, two to five feet tall, covers clear cuts and roadways at middle altitudes in the Cascades. Snowbush blooming on a hillside looks like fresh snow.

Mountain Sorrel

Snowbush

YELLOW POND LILY

The Indians called this plant wokas. Many Indian tribes, notably the Klamath Indians, depended heavily on the wokas for food. They annually trekked to the Klamath marsh to await the ripening of the seeds. They danced and held ceremonies until the seeds were ripe, and then gathered the wokas in huge hand-made sacks. The women ground most of the seeds to powder and flour; some were roasted and eaten like popcorn.

Yellow pond lilies may be observed in some ponds and lakes below timberline in Indian Heaven.

SPRING BEAUTY (Claytonia)

The stems and leaves of many claytonia have been used as food. The round basal portion of this plant, relished by the Indians, has a taste similar to radishes when eaten raw. When cooked, it tastes somewhat like a baked potato.

There are about ten species of claytonia in North America. They are widespread in the mountains of the western states and may be found in the foothills or high alpine slopes, wherever the ground is moist in the spring.

Yellow Pond Lily

Spring Beauty (Claytonia)

WILD ROSE

The Indians used the wild rose for a variety of purposes. They made a hot beverage for colds from the tender roots, they used the leaves and hips to make a drink to cure colic, and they made a mixture from the cooked seeds to alleviate muscular pains. Also, arrow shafts were made from the straight stems.

This dainty rose is fairly common in moist forest areas throughout the Cascades. Rose fruits, called hips, have been called one of the finest sources of Vitamin C available in the world. They make excellent jams and jellies, although one should wait until after the first frost before picking them.

COW PARSNIP

The huge stem of the cow parsnip is edible. It may be cut before the flowers open and, with the outer covering peeled off, sliced and prepared much like rhubarb. It may also be eaten raw. The stems are sliced into very thin pieces and used as salad greens. The Pacific Indians from Alaska to California used the tender young leaves for food. It is said that they took the basal portion of the plant, burned it, and used the ashes for salt. In addition, some Indians used a preparation made from the mashed root to alleviate a sore throat. After soaking the root in water, the resulting solution was gargled.

Wild Rose   **Cow Parsnip**

BEARGRASS

Also called squawgrass, elkgrass. The name squawgrass results from the Indians' use of the grass-like leaves for weaving baskets and clothing, the work of the squaws in the tribe. Squawgrass was so important that it was even used as an article of trade by the Indians who constructed baskets, hats, pouches, and even watertight cooking pots from the coarse leaves. The Indians often colored some of the beargrass with various plant dyes, weaving it into basket designs. The names elkgrass and beargrass come from the fact that these animals sometimes eat a great deal of this plant. Since individual plants may not bloom every year, the flowers may be abundant one year, almost absent the next.

PINEMAT MANZANITA

The Indians had many uses for the small fruits and red berries of the manzanita. They ate the berries raw, stewed, boiled, or ground into a powder. They also made a cider from them, first crushing them and adding hot water. The brew was cooled before drinking. There were still other uses for the manzanita. A solution made from the berries was used for curing poison oak and the crushed leaves were dried and mixed with tobacco for smoking. The hard wood was used by the early California settlers as pegs in place of iron nails.

Beargrass

Pinemat Manzanita

A low, sprawling red-barked shrub, seldom over a foot high, this pinemat manzanita is common from moderate altitudes to near timberline in the Cascades. It has white, urn-shaped flowers and round red berries.

There are over 45 species of manzanita and most of them occur in the Pacific Coastal states.

SERVICEBERRY

The sweet, deep blue fruit of the serviceberry was a regular part of the Indians' diet. They dried them and pounded them into cakes for use in the winter, adding small bits to soups, stews and vegetables. The Indians also made a concoction called pemmican by combining the berries with venison. This was carried on long trips and was a favorite camp ration.

The serviceberry has clusters of fragrant white blossoms in early summer followed by the dark fruit. Some find the berries mealy.

In the Cascades the serviceberry is a small tree, 15 to 20 feet tall; however, it may be more stunted at timberline.

Serviceberry

COMMON CAMAS

Common in the subalpine meadows of the Cascades, camas was one of the most important of all native plants to the Indians. Tribes cherished the onion-like root and guarded the tribal camas fields from rivals. After the seeds were ripe, bulbs were harvested and baked or roasted for at least 24 hours in a deep hole lined with stones heated in a fire. If not eaten immediately, the blackened outer covering was stripped off and the interior was pressed into a flat cake and hung to dry before storing. The bulb was also dug by the early pioneers and saved many from starvation. In California, settlers made pies from the camas bulb. After stewing, the bulbs took on the consistency of pumpkin.

Care was always taken when digging the camas since the poisonous "death camas" often grows with the edible camas. When flowering they are easily distinguished. The common camas has blue flowers while the death camas has pale greenish-white flowers. However, after the flowering season they look very much alike because death camas is also one to two feet tall and has grass-like leaves.

Common Camas

PART 2:
Trails

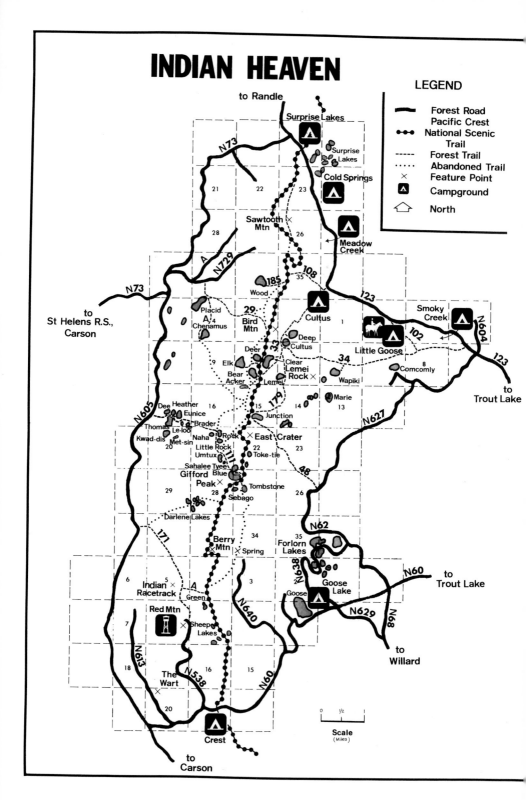

INDIAN HEAVEN

LEGEND

▬▬▬	Forest Road
●●●	Pacific Crest National Scenic Trail
- - -	Forest Trail
·····	Abandoned Trail
✕	Feature Point
🅰	Campground
⬆	North

to Randle

Surprise Lakes

Surprise Lakes

Cold Springs

N73

21   22   23

Sawtooth Mtn

28

26

Meadow Creek

108

N729

185

35

Wood

123

N73

to St Helens R.S., Carson

Placid

Chenamus

29

Bird Mtn

Cultus

1

Smoky Creek

N604

Deep Cultus

Little Goose

102

123

Deer

Clear

Lemei Rock

34

Comcomly   8

9   Elk   Lemei

Bear Acker   Lemei

Wapiki

to Trout Lake

Marie

13

Dee Heather   16

Eunice

15

179

14

Junction

N627

Thomas Le-loo

Brader

Kwad-dis   Met-sin

Naha   Rock

East Crater

20   Little Rock

Umtux

22   Toke-tie   23

N605

Sahalee Tyee

Gifford Peak   Blue

48

29   28   Tombstone

Siebago   26

Darlene Lakes

171

Berry Mtn

34   Spring   35   Forlorn Lakes   N62

6   5   Indian Racetrack   3   Goose

Green   Goose Lake

N638

N60   to Trout Lake

Red Mtn

7   Sheepe Lakes

N640   N629   N68

to Willard

N613

18   16   15

The Wart   N538   N60

20

Crest

to Carson

0   ½   1

Scale
(Miles)

34

TRAILS

Snow usually remains in the Indian Heaven back country until the middle of July. This condition may vary somewhat from year to year, but it is a good idea to plan a first trip for the latter part of July. Snow usually returns to the area anytime after November 1.

Two hazards should be considered in planning a trip too early or too late. Mosquitos rule the land immediately following the snow melt in July, and a November snow storm can cover the trail causing a hiker to become confused and lost. A good repellant should handle the mosquito problem, but snowshoes and a compass would be required to hike out of a snow storm.

Indian Heaven is beautiful at any time, but hiking is best in September and October when people are few, mosquitos are gone, fishing is great, the air is crisp and the landscape is colored with red, yellow and bronze hues.

The following trail descriptions are based upon personal observations from hiking the trails many times. In some cases, trails will be combined so the hiker can reach more points of interest on a single hike.

INDIAN RACE TRACK TRAIL NO. 171

What the Olympics mean to today's sports world, the "Race Track" meant to the Northwest Indians. It was here the tribes congregated to hold their summer celebrations as their main sport was horse racing. The track worn by the ponies' hooves is still visible. It is approximately ten feet wide, more than 2,000 feet long.

Trail No. 171 is 3.1 miles in length beginning and ending at roadsides, so you may start your hike into the race track from either end of the trail. If you wish to hike its full length, there are several options: bring two cars and leave at opposite ends of the trail; have someone drop you off at one trail head and pick you up at the other end of the trail; or hike the round trip distance of 6.2 miles. Since most people hike only as far as the race track and return to their cars, I will describe the trips into the race track from both points of entry.

The Red Mountain, or south approach, is the shortest distance to the race track, and represents a round trip hike of 1.6 miles. The trail head can be reached by driving north from Carson, Washington, to Road N605. Turn right on N605 and follow to its junction with N60. Turn right (east) on N60 and follow a short distance to its junction with N538. Turn left (north) on N538 and follow to the trail head on Red Mountain. Total driving distance from Carson is 20.5 miles and the roads are good with the exception of the last two miles. Regular passenger cars with reasonable ground clearance should negotiate the road without a problem, but ground-huggers will not clear the road centers.

The trail head can be reached also from Trout Lake, Washington. Drive west on Road 123, then N60 to the intersection of Road N538. Turn north on N538 to the trail head. The driving distance from Trout Lake is approximately 20 miles.

To find the start of the trail, look for a large signpost that may or may not have a sign on it as you round the last curve before reaching the top of the mountain. A parking spot is located across the road on the uphill side.

The trail drops off rapidly from the top of the mountain descending through Noble firs, mountain hemlocks, lodgepole pines and an occasional meadow. The upper portion of the trail allows sweeping views of nearby Berry Mountain to the north, 5,927 foot Lemei Rock and snow covered, 12,326 foot Mt. Adams to the northeast. Wild flowers bloom along the trail during each season. From the middle of July to the middle of August, columbine, heather, spreading phlox, common paintbrush and alpine shooting star are on display. In 0.8 mile the trail bursts out of the trees onto the race track meadow. Before proceeding further you should put a marker of some sort on a tree or bush to help relocate the trail for your return trip.

Indian Race Track and ice-bound Race Track Lake

Red Mountain Lookout and Mt. Hood

You will have no problem finding the race track since it stands out prominently in the meadow landscape. Two small lakes are situated near the track. The Forest Service has not given them names, nor are they stocked with fish, but the Skamania County Recreation base map calls them "Race Track Lakes." Yellow pond lilies are in bloom around the first of August. A number of primitive campsites are located near these lakes on the meadow perimeter.

The last Indian horse race was held in 1928 with the winner taking the loser's horse. Retired Forest Service employees say the race track meadow was at least twice as big then as it is now. Trees have gradually taken over much of the area. The western end of the race track was, in fact, lost in the trees until a group of history minded citizens quietly removed them in 1976. Old timers say the track groove is not as deep as it used to be due to soil build-up from decaying vegetation. Be that as it may, the race track is still a place to gratify your love of history.

The return trip is a tough uphill climb, so take lots of rest stops, enjoy the views from the upper part of the trail, and look forward to a surprise reward when the hike is over, the fabulous view from the top of the 4,968 foot Red Mountain Cinder Cone. The old lookout tower is up the road 0.2 mile from where you parked your car, so drive on up, climb the steps to the platform and hang on. Five snow capped giants can be seen on a clear day: Mt. Jefferson and Mt. Hood in Oregon and Mt. St. Helens, Mt. Adams and Mt. Rainier in Washington. These mountains, plus dozens of smaller peaks and hundreds of square miles of forest land, make a view worth the trip even if you do not hike into the race track.

The second trail approach to the race track originates at Falls Creek. The trail head can be reached by driving north from Carson, Washington, to Road N605. Turn right on N605 and follow all the way to the trail head just north of Falls Creek. Total driving distance from Carson is 21.2 miles.

This trail head can be reached also from Trout Lake, Washington. Drive west on Road 123, then N60 to the intersection with Road N605. Turn north on N605 to the trail sign. Total driving distance from Trout Lake is approximately 24 miles.

The trail commences on near level terrain for the first 0.2 mile. At that point you must ford Falls Creek. By mid-July the creek depth is usually low enough to expose stepping stones, so you should have no problem crossing. Fill your canteen here. Tighten your belt upon reaching the other side because the trail proceeds at a jet takeoff rate for the next three-fourths of a mile. On this section of the trail you will pass through a forest of true fir and mountain hemlock. From mid-July to mid-August, columbine, low mountain lupine, subalpine buttercup, and beargrass bloom along the trail.

In the fall of the year you should be on the alert for bears as there is a healthy population in this section of Indian Heaven. If you do not see any I can almost guarantee you will see their huckleberry filled scat on the trail. Be sure and remember to shout periodically so that mama bear will have advance notice to move her cubs out of the area.

The trail continues to climb gradually through noble fir and lodge-pole pine all the way to the race track. You will have hiked 2.3 tough miles when you reach your destination and will welcome the chance to rest, relax and observe the track. Your return trip to the car will be an easy downhill trek. The total round trip distance is 4.6 miles.

For those who wish to hike the entire 3.1 mile trail from one end to the other, I recommend starting from the Red Mountain trail head because the trail from this point is downhill all the way descending from approximately 4,950 feet to 3,600 feet. Allowing liberal time for observing the race track, you can hike it in less than two and one-half hours.

I will always remember my first hike into this Indian paradise. It was during the fall of the year and the landscape had taken on its yellow, brown and red hues in preparation for the dormant season. The race track meadow was enshrouded by rolling fog and the scene gave forth an eerie feeling as I thought back in time to the thousands of Indians who were once here. I stood by the race track and visualized the track lined with Indian spectators cheering on their favorite horse and rider. I looked around the surrounding meadow and saw the hundreds of tepees and campfires. I observed the women tanning the hides, drying the huckleberries and weaving the baskets. I saw the men seated in groups across from each other playing the hide and point hand game "chall-chall." It's now all a matter of history to be relived only in one's imagination.

To see the race track is an experience I will always remember; you will, too.

THOMAS LAKE TRAIL NO. 111

More than twenty lovely lakes and tarns lie alongside or just off the trail on this 3.3 mile scenic trip into the Indian Heaven back country. The deep color hues of one, Blue Lake, rival the beauty of Oregon's renowned Crater Lake. Another, Rock Lake, nestles in a large alpine meadow sufficient to house a football stadium, and a viewer might wonder if landscape artists had placed the huge boulders around the lake's perimeter. A third, Sahalee-Tyee, is thought to be the round bowl of an extinct volcanic crater. It is an absolutely lovely trail and the high meadow sections, in particular, will charm the viewer with their unique kind of scenic beauty.

The trail head can be reached by driving north from Carson to Road N605. Turn right on N605 and follow all the way to the trail sign. Total driving distance from Carson is approximately 24.5 miles.

The trail head can be reached also from Trout Lake. Drive west on Road 123, then N60 to the intersection with Road N605. Turn north on N605 to the trail sign. Total driving distance from Trout Lake is approximately 27.4 miles.

Until recent years the trail was known as "Brader Way." John Brader, an old sheepherder, somehow got his name on it as well as on one of the off-trail lakes. Sheepherders were allowed to graze their flocks in the high meadows until 1944 and it is presumed that is how Brader's name became associated with the area. Originally, the trail extended west from the old Pacific Crest Trail, but only as far as Thomas Lake. It was not until the early 1970's that the Forest Service brought the trail out to Road N605. Now you can visit five of the lakes on a short 1.2 mile round trip hike that very young and older citizens should handle with ease.

Thomas Lake

Blue Lake

The setting of the trail head is typical of so many others in Indian Heaven, with huckleberry brush, bear grass and wild flower ground cover under an umbrella of coniferous trees.

The trail starts with a gradual ascent that continues to the first group of lakes. The elevation gain is approximately 300 feet in 0.6 mile. The first lake to come into view is Dee Lake, a small but pretty lake stocked with cutthroat trout. Thomas Lake appears almost simultaneously on the opposite (south) side of the trail. Thomas is the largest and most scenic of this group of lakes. It covers 10.5 acres and is stocked with both brook and cutthroat trout. Some fishermen claim to have also caught Montana black spotted trout from Thomas Lake. If this is true, the fish are carry-overs from early plants. A short side trip will bring you to 3.5 acre Kwad-dis Lake. Hike south on the westerly shore line of Thomas Lake and you will find Kwad-dis lying immediately contiguous to Thomas on the south end. There is no trail here but it is easy going. Kwad-dis is an Indian Chinook word meaning "The Whale." The State Game Department does not plant fish in Kwad-dis Lake, but I have thought about casting a line and lure to determine whether it, too, might hold Montana black spotted trout from early plants.

Trail 111 continues east from Thomas Lake with Heather Lake appearing immediately on the left (north) side of the trail. This scenic three acre lake is stocked with cutthroat trout.

The trail turns abruptly south at the east end of Heather Lake; however, you can visit still another lake by continuing easterly on Trail 111A for approximately 250 yards beyond the trail junction. This short side trip leads to Eunice Lake, six acres in size and 22 feet deep. The lake holds cutthroat trout.

Some fishermen bring in light rubber rafts to get them out into the deep water of these lakes.

All five lakes lie at approximately 4,400 feet elevation.

Primitive campsites can be found on the western and eastern shores of Thomas Lake and the western shore of Eunice Lake. Another semi-improved site is located in sight of the trail between Heather and Thomas lakes.

With this enjoyable but easy part of the hike completed, you are now ready to move into the high country beyond. Brace yourself, because the next 0.2 mile is a mountain goat climb. The trail ascends south and then east allowing views of Eunice Lake far below to the north.

The path levels out abruptly at the end of the climb and turns sharply to the east (right). Hike about 200 feet down the trail and look to the south (right) for an opening in the trees. Walk, cross country, about 600 feet in the direction of the opening into a beautiful meadow carpeted with mountain heather, low huckleberry brush and wild flowers. Walk through the meadow in an easterly direction (left) to "Lake Le-Loo" (the big grey wolf). A game trail leads from the meadow to the lake and you may see tracks of elk, deer and wildcat along the lake shore. I saw no evidence that man had been in this place in recent years, and I presume that is why the animals love the area.

Another lake called "La Met-Sin" (medicine) is located a short distance southwest of Lake Le-Loo but I do not recommend this hike unless you are thoroughly familiar with maps and compass. The word La Met-Sin indicates the influence of early French explorers and the Indians' attempt to pronounce the word medicine.

Trail 111 continues on a near flat grade, passes through another luscious meadow and proceeds with a moderate ascent to a lakelet lying on the left (north) side of the trail. At this point look for a sign "Brader Lake" posted on a tree to the right side of the trail. Brader Lake is located out of sight, over a ridge about 200 yards south of the trail. It is a beautiful three acre lake lying at an elevation of 4,600 feet. A short trail should be built to it. Some old maps call it Broder Lake in error. I have not been able to ascertain if it holds fish.

From Brader Lake, the going gets a little tougher with a 200 foot elevation gain to Rock Lake in 0.7 mile. The trail is badly rutted in places from horse traffic, and you may need to walk to the side of the trail part of the way.

You should be encouraged when you pass a large rock slide because you are now nearing Naha Lake and the hard part of the hike will soon be over. Rock Lake lies just beyond.

Naha Lake possesses an unforgettable charm. It lies at an elevation of 4,740 feet, is half an acre in size and only seven feet deep. Somehow the setting and the trees around it make you want to take its picture immediately. "Naha" means "mother" in Chinook. Some old maps show it as Nahe Lake.

In 0.1 mile from Naha Lake you will arrive at Rock Lake, thus completing the first 2.1 miles of your trip.

I do not know how many times I have drifted to sleep while visualizing the beauty of Rock Lake, the large boulders protruding above the water on its perimeter; the diminutive Noble firs, the huge meadows around it, the greens of summer, and the golds, yellows and browns of fall. Rock Lake possesses a mystique all its own.

The country from Rock Lake to Blue Lake is intoxicating. To experience it, turn south (right) near the western edge of Rock Lake and pick up the trail. You may have some trouble finding it as hikers have a tendency to disperse in the meadows and no real trail is established. It does become prominent, however, as you approach Little Rock Lake which is located immediately south of Rock Lake.

Little Rock Lake is the baby sister of Rock Lake. It has all the characteristics of Rock Lake including the boulders, Noble fir, and the surrounding meadows.

The trail proceeds in a southeasterly direction into a paradise of small lakes, park-like meadows with wild flowers, and alpine scenery that will leave you spellbound.

Umtux Lake (named after an Indian chief) is actually the general name used for 13 lakes located on or near the trail extending from Little Rock Lake to the intersection with a recently abandoned portion of the Pacific Crest National Scenic Trail. This 0.7 mile section is surely as photographic as any wilderness area anywhere. It is here you will observe isolated earth mounds in the meadows, each mound alive with dwarf Noble fir, low huckleberry brush and wild flowers giving forth the appearance of a miniature Japanese garden. October is the month to see them in their most colorful dress.

If you wish to find the off-trail Umtux lakes use your compass together with the Topographic map produced by the U.S. Geological Survey. The map you need is the Wind River, Washington, Skamania County.

The trail now continues on a downgrade and arrives at Sahalee-Tyee (great spirit) Lake in 0.3 mile. Because of its round appearance, Sahalee-Tyee is thought to lie in the bowl of an extinct volcanic crater. It is seven acres in size, more than 25 feet deep and holds both cutthroat and brook trout. A near-level campsite is located near the western shore about 50 feet off the trail. In the past it has been called several names such as Round Lake, Indian Heaven Lake and Green Lake. It is located at an elevation of 4,700 feet, down 100 feet from Rock Lake. It is interesting to observe the changes in this 100 foot drop in elevation. The meadows gradually disappear, giving way to the forest.

The trail proceeds on a downward, southeasterly course and in about 0.2 mile parallels Blue Lake along its eastern shore to the intersection with the Pacific Crest National Scenic Trail near the southeast end of the lake.

I hope it is a clear, calm day when you first view Blue Lake. The deep blue coloring is a rich cobalt hue, and the view of 5,368 foot Gifford Peak sweeping upward 728 feet from its shore line is a sight to behold.

Blue Lake lies at an elevation of 4,640 feet, is 12 acres in size, 46-some feet deep, and holds both brook and cutthroat trout. A small campsite is located on the east side near the trail, but the main camp area is located at the southeast end of the lake where there is space for 10 camps. Another site is located on a small peninsula of land which juts into the lake west of the main camp.

This marks the end of Trail 111, but it would be a shame not to visit Tombstone Lake since you have already come this far. Tombstone Lake is just a 0.2 mile downhill hike from the camp area. (Disregard the old ½ mile sign.)

Tombstone Lake got its name from a huge stone which rears out of the water near its easterly shore line. The stone is shaped remarkably like a tombstone you might see in an old churchyard cemetery.

The return trip will be easier than your trip in. It is an ascent of 160 feet to Rock Lake and a drop of approximately 740 feet to Road N605. Take careful watch of your direction at Rock Lake because the trail turns abruptly west at that point and a continued northerly course would place you on the **original** Crest Trail and lead you astray to the northeast. If you do not pass by Naha Lake within three or four minutes after leaving Rock Lake, you will know you have headed the wrong way.

Trail 111 represents a round trip hike of 6.8 miles without side trips such as Kwad-dis Lake, Eunice Lake, Lake Le-Loo, Tombstone Lake, or any of the off-trail Umtux lakes. You should allow at least five hours so that you do not over extend yourself and so that you can enjoy a leisurely lunch somewhere along the way.

I have hiked this trail a number of times with companions who continue to ask me to take them along the next time I go. Trail 111 (Thomas Lake) is just that kind of a trail. There is enough magic up there to keep you coming back time after time.

Earth mound gardens are a phenomenon along trail between Little
Rock Lake and Old Crest Trail junction

Rock Lake

LEMEI TRAIL NO. 34

The grandeur of the views and the contrasts of nature make this 5.2 mile trail an experience that remains long in one's memory. It is a place of lakes, of volcanic craters and of bright meadows. It is a place of bald eagles and hoary marmots. Views of Mt. Rainier, Mt. Adams, the Goat Rocks, Sleeping Beauty and Sawtooth Mountain seem to explode through openings in the trees and from the high meadows. Wapiki Lake sparkles like a blue jewel when viewed from the upper rim of the volcanic crater in which it lies. Massive pinnacles of 5,927 foot Lemei Rock Mountain tower overhead as the trail meanders 300 feet beneath. High meadows proudly display their colorful wild flowers in park-like wonderlands.

The trail commences at a point just southeast of the Smoky Creek Campground on Road 123. I prefer, however, to start the hike from Little Goose Campground because the Filloon Trail No. 102 from this camp intersects the trail we are describing in 0.9 mile and saves 0.4 mile of uphill climbing.

To reach Little Goose Campground and the trail head, drive north-west from Carson, Washington, on the Wind River Highway, then northeast on Road N73 to the end of the pavement. Angle right and continue on N73 to the Sawtooth huckleberry fields. Turn right (south) on Road 123 to the campground. The distance from Carson is approximately 39.3 miles.

The Little Goose trail head can be reached also from Trout Lake, Washington. Drive west and north on Road 123 to the campground in approximately 15.5 miles.

The trail head is located at the back end of a 0.2 mile dead-end road that extends through the campground. A horse camp is located here with unloading facilities and a corral. Park your car away from the road circle and the unloading ramp. The trail sign "Filloon Trail No. 102" is prominently displayed at the south end of the road circle. This trail was named for the late Ray Filloon who managed the Cultus Creek Guard Station for many years and whose outstanding photography has been enjoyed by thousands.

The path commences its magic course through an amazing combination of trees. Alder and other deciduous trees usually found at lower elevations grow alongside Noble firs, mountain hemlocks and white pines. The ground cover is predominantly bear grass (squaw grass) and huckleberry brush. Wild flowers bloom as soon as the snow melts in July and continue to bloom into early September. It is unfortunate that the flower season is also the mosquito season, so come prepared with repellent.

46

n 0.9 mile the trail intersects Lemei Trail No. 34 which leads to the alpine paradise beyond. Prepare yourself for the climb of your life because the trail now commences an unmerciful ascent of 1,440 feet in less than 3.0 miles.

At approximately 0.7 mile from the trail intersection, the subalpine zone is apparent and deciduous trees are left behind. Trail switchbacks start negotiating the steep terrain in quick succession and you must watch your footing carefully on some rough sections of the trail. In another 0.3 mile a parade of views commences. Mt. Adams appears to the northeast and the Goat Rocks appear to the north of Mt. Adams. Sleeping Beauty Mountain can be seen to the south of Mt. Adams. Miles of green forest floor provide a thrilling foreground to these mountains and snowcapped volcanoes. Mini meadows soon provide further tree openings which allow additional views of Sawtooth Mountain and Mt. Rainier to the north.

At 2.6 miles from the Little Goose Campground the trail intersects the Wapiki Lake Trail. This trail is missing from the Gifford Pinchot National Forest Service map, but is shown on the map enclosed in this book. It is not maintained, but is well used and easy to follow. You should definitely take this 0.3 mile side trail as it leads to one of the highlights of your trip.

Wapiki Lake is a calendar-cover scene. It lies in the bowl of an extinct volcanic crater, is ten plus acres in area and stocked with cutthroat trout. Parts of its shoreline are open meadows. Primitive campsites are located on the south side of the lake. Three small lakelets are located close by to the south of Wapiki and three more are located to the southwest.

The main trail continues near-vertical to the top of the crater rim above Wapiki. The view of the lake from this overlook is sure to draw gasps. For many years the Forest Service has planned geological interpretive signing on this overlook, but the sign has never been installed.

The path crosses the high cindered crater rim and wanders beneath the rugged pinnacles of Lemei Rock Mountain. Only experienced mountain climbers with rock climbing equipment should attempt to climb Lemei Rock at this point. The true 5,925 foot summit should be approached from a natural grade commencing one-half mile further along the trail. The route is obvious to the eye, but a compass should be used to maintain direction on the lower forested slopes.

Lemei Rock is the highest point in Indian Heaven, and the views from the summit are unbelievable. A complete circle turn will reveal

The vast amphitheater of Lemei Rock Mountain, Lemei Crater and Wapiki Lake

sweeping vistas that will remain indelible in your memory for as long as you live — views that reach out beyond Mt. Rainier, Mt. Adams, Mt. St. Helens and Mt. Hood — views that extend into the dry lands of eastern Washington and Oregon.

Eagles and hoary marmots inhabit Lemei Rock. On one trip I watched a bald eagle spiral upward on an elevator of hot air, then sweep off and plummet toward an unseen prey. I also observed hoary marmots sunning themselves on a southern slope.

The trail proceeds past Lemei Rock in a northwesterly direction and continues on a downward course through meadow park lands. The variety of wild flowers is dazzling from snow melt through August.

Presuming that you took the side trip into Wapiki Lake, you will have traveled 5.4 miles upon your arrival at Cultus Lake and the intersection with the Indian Heaven Trail No. 33.

Cultus (bad lake) appears the opposite of its name. It is cobalt blue in color and is surrounded by tree studded meadows. The reason it got its name is because the Indians believed that Big Foot (Sasquatch) inhabited the area. The lake is stocked with cutthroat trout. A near-level campsite is located near the southwest shore line.

A full day should be allowed to complete this 10.8 mile round trip hike. You can avoid the long retracing of Trail 34 and Trail 102 by going out from Cultus Lake by way of Trail 33 to the Cultus Creek Campground. In the process you will save 2.3 hiking miles, but a second car will be required to take you back to your first car at the Little Goose trail head.

I am sure you will find this trip a rich and rewarding wild experience. How did I feel as I first concluded the hike? The same as now — I've got to get back into that country!

INDIAN HEAVEN TRAIL NO. 33 (Sahalee-Tyee)

Most appropriately named is this fascinating trail that winds into the alpine wilderness of lakes and meadows from the Cultus Creek Campground. Three of the larger Indian Heaven lakes lie alongside the trail and four others can be reached by short side trails. Each lake is tucked away in its own, special, scenic setting and all but one contain fish. The upper part of the trail passes through meadow after meadow and finally along meadows so large they could accommodate a small town. These are luscious, flower carpeted meadows from mid-July to September, and crimson and golden hued meadows from mid-September to November. The area the trail covers is a photographer's dream.

Cultus Lake

Clear Lake Meadow

Deep Lake (opposite)

The trail head at Cultus Creek Campground can be reached from Carson by driving north on the Wind River Highway, then northeast on Road N73 to the end of the pavement. Angle right and continue on Road N73 to the Sawtooth huckleberry fields. Turn south (right) on Road 123 to the campground. Driving distance from Carson is approximately 37 miles.

From Trout Lake, drive Road 123 to the campground in approximately 18 miles. Park your car in the area signed "Parking for Hikers" just inside and to the right of the campground entrance.

The trail head is located about half way around the in-and-out road loop on the west side (right) of the road. Another trail, Cultus Creek Trail No. 108, also originates from this campground so be sure and read the sign before starting up the trail.

If you are going on horseback do not plan to leave your animals in the campground overnight. Ingress and egress only is the rule.

The first 1.7 miles of the Indian Heaven Trail is the hurdle you must overcome to enjoy the meadows and lakes beyond. You will not find a level spot for a breather until you have climbed through heavy forest from 3,988 feet elevation to 5,000 feet. This difficult stretch of trail has caused many people to turn back short and miss the scenic thrills of the back country. My sincere advice is to take it easy, but keep going, because you will be glad you did once you get on top.

Once on top, start looking for a trail sign "Deep Lake." This side trail leads to one of the prettiest lakes in Indian Heaven. The trail mileage on the sign is actually in error; true distance is closer to 0.2 mile rather than 0.5 mile.

Deep Lake lies at an elevation of 5,083 feet. (U.S.G.S. Lone Butte, Washington.) The water depth is in excess of 25 feet and the lake area covers six acres. Both brook and cutthroat trout abound in its cool water, and some reports have it that rainbow trout also thrive here as hold-overs from fish plants of early years. The side trail into the lake arrives on the western shore and the view to the east is phenomenal. Massive Mt. Adams thrusts her snow covered head above the lake and the trees to create a scene you will want to feature prominently in your photo album. Undeveloped campsites are spotted around the lake, but the best site is located on the north shore where a huge rock, with a relatively flat top, extends into the lake. No danger of uncontrolled fire here!

The main trail continues southwesterly and arrives at Cultus Lake in another 0.2 mile. Indian paintbrush grow together with other wild flowers along this section of the trail.

Cultus (bad) Lake lies at an elevation of 5,000 feet, is four acres in area and contains cutthroat trout. The water color is deep blue, and the scattered alpine trees and the meadow around the shore give the lake a distinct personality.

The trail skirts the shore line and arrives in 0.1 mile at the intersection with Lemei Trail No. 34 on the southwest side of the lake. The best campsite around Cultus is located approximately 250 feet up Trail 34 on the south side of the lake. From this camp you can view 5,706 foot Bird Mountain to the northwest and 5,927 foot Lemei Rock Mountain to the southeast.

The path proceeds 0.3 mile through mini meadows and alongside tarns to its intersection with the Lemei Lake Trail No. 179. Look to the left for your first view of one of Indian Heaven's huge meadows. This one could accommodate a Grecian coliseum with parking space for a thousand chariots.

The trail borders the meadow for about 0.1 mile and arrives near the northeast end of Clear Lake. A sign points down a short side trail to the lake. A better view of the lake is located another 0.5 mile down the trail on the south side of the lake.

Clear Lake is situated at 4,800 foot elevation, is 13 acres in area, over 30 feet deep and holds both brook and cutthroat trout. Many years ago the lake was called "Slide Lake" because of the mammoth rock slide rising above its north shore line.

From Clear Lake the trail drops down 0.3 mile to the junction with the Pacific Crest National Scenic Trail No. 2000, about 200 feet southeast of Bear Lake. (This new section of the Crest Trail was completed in 1977.)

Bear Lake, somehow, projects an aura of mystery. Perhaps this is partly due to its name and partly due to the way the heavy forest closes in around the shore line. To me the lake is both beautiful and foreboding. It lies at an elevation of 4,750 feet, is six acres in area, more than 32 feet deep and holds both brook and cutthroat trout. Several campsites are located around the lake. One is situated on a peninsula of land extending into the water on the southeast end. Another is across the lake on the west side and a third is located on the northwest end of the lake adjacent to the old Crest Trail.

The trail continues southwest beyond the Pacific Crest National

Clear Lake
Bear Lake

Fall colors border meadow south of Acker Lake (opposite)

Scenic Trail No. 2000, skirts Bear Lake and ends at the intersection of the old Crest Trail in about 0.4 mile. You need not stop here, because there is more to see close by if you have the inclination and the time. You can hike either south or north on the old Crest Trail and view additional lakes and meadows.

A short 400 foot walk south (left) will bring you to Acker Lake and another 0.4 mile will show you some of the largest and grandest meadows in Indian Heaven. A view of those meadows is a must.

Acker Lake (not shown on the Forest Service map) is a little jewel. It is only 1.5 acres in size, but situated in a setting that makes you want to linger. The 4,650 foot high meadow which partially surrounds it is covered with mountain heather and sprinkled with wild flowers. A good campsite is located just off the trail near the southeast shore. The lake was named after George Acker of Carson. Do not confuse Acker Lake with the unnamed lake lying across the trail to the east.

A walk north (right) of the trail junction will take you to two more lakes. Follow the old Crest Trail for 0.4 mile to a side trail sign which reads "Elk Lake." Look for the tree sign just north of Bear Lake. The trail into the lake is 0.2 mile.

Elk Lake is 13 acres in area, over 17 feet deep and contains both brook and cutthroat trout. It lies at an elevation of 4,685 feet.

If you still have time continue north on the old Crest Trail to Deer Lake. You will pass by an interconnecting trail to the new Pacific Crest Trail in 0.1 mile and arrive at Deer Lake in another 0.3 mile.

Deer Lake lies at an elevation of 4,800 feet, is 5.5 acres in size and holds both brook and cutthroat trout. A campsite with space for four or more tents is located on the western shore.

You should allow a full day to enjoy the Indian Heaven Trail. The round trip hiking distance will be approximately 7.6 miles if you include the side trip into Deep Lake, and approximately 10.4 miles if you include both south and north side trips on the old Crest Trail.

In October of 1976, I hiked the trail for the third time with a group of friends. I enjoyed pointing out places of interest as we moved along the trail. Mother Nature had clothed the landscape in its fall dress and the beauty of the country was staggering. I happened to notice tears in the eyes of one of my companions. I asked her, "Is something wrong?" She replied, "No, it's all so beautiful I can't keep from crying." Indian Heaven Trail No. 33 can do that to you.

CULTUS CREEK TRAIL NO. 108
AND WOOD LAKE TRAIL NO. 185

Cultus Creek Trail No. 108 is not for everyone. It belongs to those who are strong of limb and stout of heart and to those willing to put forth an extra effort in order to enjoy mind-blowing views of snow-capped giants and a world of forest at their feet. It has been called "The Cardiac Arrest Trail" because a portion of it climbs a wicked 1,249 feet in just over a mile.

Wood Lake Trail No. 185 to lovely Wood Lake is the 0.5 mile trail used in combination with Trail 108 to complete the trip I will describe.

Cultus Creek Campground is the starting point for this challenging hike. Drive northwest from Carson on the Wind River Highway, then northeast on Road N73 to the end of the pavement. Angle right and continue on N73 to the Sawtooth huckleberry fields. Turn south (right) on Road 123 to the campground. Driving distance from Carson is approximately 37 miles.

The trail head may be reached also from Trout Lake. Road 123 will take you to the campground in approximately 18 miles.

The driveway in and out of the campground is a one-way loop. A sign, "Parking for Hikers," is posted adjacent to Road 123 just north of the entry. The trail sign is about 200 feet inside the entry road on the right side.

Pack animals are allowed ingress and egress through the campground to the trail head, but are not to remain in the camp overnight.

One of the fascinating things about this hike is the changing vegetation zones to be observed from the start of the trail to its highest elevation on Bird Mountain. The path enters and passes through mixed deciduous and coniferous forests to dry openings in coniferous forests to high, park-like, alpine meadows where small clumps of trees punctuate the open areas. Throughout the trail you may observe the constantly changing flowers and trees, each species growing at the elevation that suits it best.

The first one-half mile is the easiest part of the hike. You will find even an occasional semi-level spot to rest legs and lungs. Take note, as you go, of the statuesque Noble fir mixed in with the white pine, the true fir and, of all things, scrub alder. Note, also, the sudden predominance of mountain hemlock as you gain elevation. Look to your right (east) through openings in the trees for partial views of

Wood Lake

Bird Mountain and Mt. Adams

t. Adams, and to your left (west) for views of Bird Mountain. Take special note of the saddle opening in Bird Mountain, for you will be passing through it before you reach the Pacific Crest National Scenic Trail No. 2000 intersection. Pick huckleberries to your heart's content during September and the first two weeks of October.

The trail continues in long switchbacks around rock out-croppings and through meadow openings to the one mile indicator. This metal tab indicator, attached to a tree, has remained intact since the days when the Gifford Pinchot National Forest was called the Columbia National Forest. This could date back to 1911 as the Columbia National Forest map for that year shows the trail. A number of these metal signs may be observed on other Indian Heaven trails and the small trees to which they are attached attest to the slow growth of trees at these elevations.

From the one mile indicator the trail ascends in dead earnest. Your frequent rest stops are not only for survival but for enjoyment, because spectacular views of Sawtooth Mountain and Mt. Rainier burst forth to the north and a turnaround view of Mt. Adams and the Goat Rocks will just about bowl you off the trail. Mountain heather carpets the ground and their blooms provide a riot of color from July snow melt through the first part of August.

In due time you will enter the saddle in Bird Mountain (5,237 feet) and descend to the Pacific Crest National Scenic Trail No. 2000.

Bird Mountain is long and massive. It extends south to north like a giant backbone for about a mile. The true summit (5,706 feet) is located near the southwest end. No trail ascends to the summit and getting there is "rough go" from any direction. A false summit of 5,568 feet is located an estimated 400 yards south of the trail, but I cannot imagine the views from the true summit to be any more spectacular than from here. Mt. Hood and Mt. St. Helens are added to the peaks you have already viewed from the trail. A natural grade approach commences just before the trail starts its descent to the crest trail. Set your compass in a southerly direction and you should have no trouble finding the peak. Your elevation gain for this side trip will be 331 feet.

You will have hiked 1.5 trail miles when you arrive at the Pacific Crest National Scenic Trail No. 2000. Now turn left (south) and follow the crest trail for approximately 0.3 mile, then veer to your right off the crest trail. You are now on a section of the old Crest Trail which will lead to the Wood Lake Trail No. 185 in an estimated 300 feet. In 1976 the trail sign read, "Wood Lake 1/2 Mile." The true distance is a little less than that.

Wood Lake is located in a pristine setting, lovingly protected by perimeter of alpine trees. It is situated at an elevation of 4,860 feet Eastern brook trout inhabit its depths. A nice campsite is located o a peninsula of land extending from the south shore. This is the plac to linger for some fishing, swimming, wandering and lunching.

Your return trip will be a breeze: a gradual 377 foot elevation gai back to the saddle in Bird Mountain and a 1,249 foot elevatio plunge to the campground.

You will have traveled approximately 4.4 trail miles when you retur to your car. Because of the severity of the climb going in, you shoul allow at least three and a half hours traveling time.

I remember my personal thoughts after first completing this trip "Man, that was one tough hike. I'm dead-tired, but happy with collection of scenic memories sufficient to keep me going until I ca get back up there again."

PLACID LAKE TRAIL NO. 29

The very name "Placid" suggests the quiet, scenic beauty to be ob served along this trail.

Youngsters and grandparents can enjoy the easy one-half mile hike a far as the lake. There is great swimming in the shallow water near the lake shore and great picnicking in the small meadow alongside. Wild strawberries and huckleberries are plentiful to eat and migrations o forest toads can be observed. Trout wait in the lake to be caught.

Drive north from Carson on the Wind River Highway and continue northeast on Road N73 to the end of the pavement. Angle right and continue on Road N73 for 2.1 miles to road N729. Turn right (east) on Road N729 for one mile to the Placid Lake trail head sign. The distance from Carson is approximately 28.1 miles.

From Trout Lake drive west and northwest on Road 123 for 22 miles to Road N73. Turn left (southwest) on Road N73 and drive six miles to Road N729. Turn left (east) on Road N729 for one mile to the Placid Lake trail head sign. The distance from Trout Lake is approximately 29 miles.

A parking area and horse unloading ramp are located directly across the road from the trail head sign.

The trail begins with an easy walk through a forest of mountain hemlock and true fir. The ground is carpeted solid with bear (squaw) rass, and when they bloom, en masse, you can imagine you are andering through a fairyland. I have never, before, seen such a eavy concentration of bear grass in one area. You cannot always ount on seeing them in bloom, however, because they do not flower very year. The blooms may be abundant one year and almost absent ae next. During August, 1974, for example, they flowered pro-asely, but were totally absent in 1975 and 1976.

arge owls live in the vicinity of Placid Lake. You may observe them erched in trees a short distance from the trail. Be careful if you ring a small dog along. A friend saved mine by picking him up at the ast second as a huge owl, talons open, swooped toward him.

he near-level trail starts a descent to the lake in about 0.4 mile and nters a mini meadow near the lake shore at 0.5 mile. A nice, un-eveloped campsite is located here with space for several tents. Colorful wild flowers pepper the ground from snow melt until late August.

'lacid Lake is super beautiful, being surrounded, for the most part, by stately, sub-alpine trees. It lies at an elevation of 4,042 feet U.S.G.S. Lone Butte, Washington), is 19.2 acres in area, and stocked with brook and cutthroat trout. Some hikers pack in light canoes or ubber rafts to assist them in reaching the deeper fishing waters. Motor powered watercraft and the landing of float planes is pro-ibited.

An unmaintained trail winds around the lake — look for swimming parades of baby forest toads just off shore and for elk, deer and cat racks along the south shore.

Trail 29 continues in a southeasterly direction across the north end of Placid Lake. You may have noticed the trail fork to your left just before you arrived at the lake. It passes by the intersection with Trail 29A in 0.1 mile and moves straight ahead, southeasterly.

The trail has been kind up to now, but its mood is about to change. I hope you are in good physical condition because you are about to climb 950 feet in 1.4 miles before you arrive at the Pacific Crest National Scenic Trail No. 2000 near Bird Mountain.

The rate of ascent is gradual for the first 0.3 mile but becomes a 'bear-cat'' thereafter. If you have ever hiked a trail where you stared directly into the ongoing trail at eye level, then looked near vertical to see nothing but endless trail above you, you will know what I mean. Rest stops become frequent for comfort and more frequent for survival.

In exactly 1.2 miles from Placid Lake you will observe a trail for with one section heading in a northeasterly direction. This trail join the Pacific Crest National Scenic Trail at a point farther north tha the route you are traveling.

I observed a trail sign at this junction that warmed my heart. It wa lying on the ground, old and beautiful. It read, "To Bear Way." Th old Crest Trail was called Bear Way back in the days of the Columbi National Forest before the year 1949. I later checked old Columbi National Forest maps and discovered that the trail we are describin was shown on the map for the year 1922. Who knows how old th sign really is! I am proud of those recreationists who left the sig alone.

The trail continues northeasterly from the junction and moves into meadow in 0.1 mile. This meadow is one of the prettiest in thi section of Indian Heaven, being bordered by a spectacular stand o Noble fir ranging in size from young babies to old granddads.

The path moves through the meadow for another 0.1 mile and arrive at the Pacific Crest National Scenic Trail No. 2000. This trail junc tion marks the official end of Trail 29.

The return trip is a downhill affair as far as Placid Lake, and near-level hike out to the trail head. The round trip travel distance i exactly four miles, and 2½ hours should be allowed to complete th hike.

Placid Lak

I must be honest and say that I would rather hike the steep part of Trail No. 29 in reverse. This can be accomplished by taking a route I will describe in *Full Loop Trail No. 1.*

The Forest Service plans to eventually re-route Trail 29 from Placid Lake to the Pacific Crest National Scenic Trail No. 2000 via Wood Lake. The new trail will eliminate much of the excessive grade on the present trail, allow for the convenient enjoyment of Wood Lake, and provide the hiker with some of those exploding views from Trail 108 on Bird Mountain.

CHENAMUS LAKE TRAIL NO. 29A

The Chenamus Lake Trail will lead you into the heart of the Indian Heaven park lands. You will pass Placid Lake, Chenamus Lake and a half dozen smaller lakes en route and you will gaze in wonder at the variety of colorful wild flowers along the way. Be sure to bring a compass because many exciting off-trail places await exploration.

The path commences at the northeast end of Placid Lake. A 0.6 mile hike on the Placid Lake Trail 29 will bring you to the trail head.

Drive north from Carson on the Wind River Highway and continue northeast on Road N73 to the end of the pavement. Angle right and continue on Road N73 for 2.1 miles to Road N729. Turn right (east) on Road N729 for one mile to the Placid Lake trail head sign. The distance from Carson is approximately 28.1 miles.

From Trout Lake, drive west and northwest on Road 123 for 22

East Crater Bowl, with ice on meadow pond *(See page 66)*

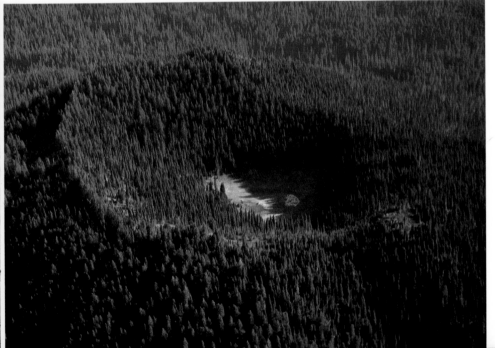

miles to Road N73. Turn left (southwest) on Road N73 and drive six miles to Road N729. Turn left (east) on Road N729 for one mile to the Placid Lake trail head sign. The distance from Carson is approximately 29 miles.

A parking area and horse unloading ramp are located directly across the road from the trail head sign.

The 0.5 mile hike into Placid Lake is a breeze. The trail turns southeasterly (left) just short of the lake and arrives at the Chenamus Lake trail head in 0.1 mile.

The path starts south through a forest of sub-alpine trees. Bear grass, vanilla leaf, the common paintbrush, bunchberries, large purple fleabanes and avalanche lilies are everywhere along the trail. Their colorful display occurs from the snow melt in July into late August. Bring mosquito repellent during this period because mosquitos "bomb" when wild flowers bloom.

The trail climbs steadily with an elevation gain of 158 feet in 0.5 mile. It levels out for the next 0.5 mile, crosses the Chenamus Lake outlet, proceeds through a mini meadow and arrives at Chenamus Lake.

According to the U.S. Geological Survey, Lone Butte, Washington, Chenamus Lake lies at an elevation of 4,245 feet and is four acres in area. This is another lake without fish. It is a pretty but lonely place. Here you will catch your first glimpse of mountain heather and alpine shooting stars which grow near the shore line. You will have to hunt to find a camping spot back in the trees.

The Forest Service maintains the trail as far as Chenamus Lake, but has abandoned the next two miles which extend to the old Crest Trail. Horses' hooves have taken their toll and I presume this is the reason the Forest Service removed the trail from inventory. The path is easy to follow; however, periodic log-stepping and puddle-jumping is required. This situation is unfortunate because the trail's approach to the Indian Heaven interior is the most gradual of all the approach trails. A new trail should be relocated along the same general location and route.

From Chenamus Lake the trail proceeds in a southeasterly direction. Follow the shore line south, then southeast, to pick up the trail. The going becomes more strenuous in the next 0.5 mile with an elevation gain of 155 feet. The trail passes alongside a lovely lake sufficient in size to make you wonder why it has not been named. However, Indian Heaven contains dozens of unnamed lakes.

Beyond the lake the trail is easy going for approximately one mile to Rush Creek. There may be a problem in fording the creek during July or August, but the stream bed is usually dry by the first of September.

The country commences to open up beyond Rush Creek. Heavy stands of sub-alpine timber gradually give way to meadow park land. Lake after lake is hidden to the west and southwest of the trail. You could spend several days searching them out with map and compass. (Use the U.S.G.S. Lone Butte, Washington map.)

Suddenly the huge Indian Heaven meadows appear in front of you and you realize what the trip has been all about. The spectacle is overwhelming.

Crossing these meadows to the intersection with the old Crest Trail could pose a problem. Hikers tend to disperse through the meadows and no real trail is established. The Forest Service installed several orange painted posts to serve as a guide, but these can become confusing because other nearby posts are directing hikers and riders from another trail originating at Rock Lake. Both trails converge like the point of a triangle and intersect at the old Crest Trail.*

Some thoughtful person erected a dead tree limb with a white cloth attached to its top. There is no guarantee it is still there, but it did mark the intersection of the trail with the old Crest Trail where you want to go. The point of intersection is 0.5 mile northwest of Junction Lake and 0.6 mile south of Acker Lake.

The trail intersection marks the end of the Chenamus Lake Trail No. 29A (formerly Placid Lake Way). The round trip is a long seven miles, so you had better allow most of a day for the outing.

The map at the front of the trail section will suggest many places to go beyond the end of the trail, but these excursions should be included in a camping trip from a base camp.

I set up a base camp at Acker Lake during October, 1976, where I stayed for several days and explored a lot of the country. One night as I stood in the calm looking into the meadows, I could almost believe that no man had ever walked on them. The Indian Heaven meadows are unbelievable, even after you have seen and walked on them.

---

*The Forest Service may remove guide posts from abandoned trails. If the posts are missing, hikers must look for the trail commencement at the meadow's edge.

EAST CRATER TRAIL NO. 48

This trail will get you started on a trip into another world, an eerie adventure into the bowl of an extinct volcanic crater. You will climb to the top of the crater rim at 5,301 feet and drop down 375 feet to the center of the crater's bowl. You may observe hoary marmots sunning themselves on the cindered slopes. The uniqueness of the experience will leave you "turned on," particularly if you have a thing about geology.

Drive north from Carson to Road N605 and follow it to Road N60. Turn right (northeast) and follow N60 to Road N629. Turn left (north) and follow to Road N638. Turn right (east) and follow to Road N62. Turn left (north) and follow for one-half mile. At this point, Road N62 becomes Road N627 and continues to the trail head in 1.3 miles. Driving distance from Carson is approximately 28.5 miles. These directions may seem complicated but the roads are well signed and easy to follow.

From Trout Lake, drive west on Road 123, then N60 to N629. Turn right (north) and follow to N638. Turn right (east) and follow to N62. Turn left (north) and follow for one-half mile. At this point, Road N62 becomes Road N627 and continues to the trail head in 1.3 miles. Driving distance from Trout Lake is approximately 18.2 miles.

The distance could have been shortened from Trout Lake by directing you north on road N62, but then you would miss the delightful drive through the Forlorn Lakes.

The trail commences at an elevation of 4,100 feet. It climbs through a heavy forest of mountain hemlock for the first 1.3 miles. The next 1.2 miles to Junction Lake is easy going through colorful meadows and alongside tarns.

The ground cover along the heavily forested section of the trail is predominantly bear (squaw) grass and huckleberry brush. Wild flowers appear in the meadows of the upper section. Mountain hemlock trees become noticeably smaller as the trail climbs and they are soon joined by Noble and true fir trees.

Junction Lake is an important point in the Indian Heaven trail system. Five trails come together here, and two others are just 0.5 mile away. The lake is situated at an elevation of 4,730 feet according to the U.S. Geological Survey, Lone Butte, Washington, and is eight acres in area. It has not been stocked with fish. Good campsites are located at the northwest end where the sandy-shored lake makes a long, narrow, extension into the meadow. Do not be deceived by the shallow appearance of the water at this point because a drop-off occurs about halfway across that will put a swimmer in over his head.

Spencer Frey of Trout Lake laughingly recalls his attempt to wade this narrow part of the lake on horseback in order to shortcut the trail. "Before I knew it my horse dropped from under me and I was up to my waist in water."

Junction Lake marks the official end of the East Crater Trail; however, the excitement and the intrigue only begin here. You can set up camp and spend a week exploring all the trails originating from this location. You might, for example, hike east and north 1.8 mile on the Lemei Lake Trail to the Indian Heaven Trail No. 33, then southwest past Clear Lake and Bear Lake to the old Crest Trail (bypass the new Pacific Crest Trail), then south past Acker Lake and through the grand Indian Heaven meadows to camp. This loop trip represents about 4.1 trail miles of easy hiking with indescribable beauty all along the way.

The map will suggest several other excursions which can be made from a base camp at Junction Lake. Some of these trails will be covered under separate headings.

A trip into East Crater must not be attempted except on a clear day. The hike is a cross country attempt that could lead into a lot of trouble on a foggy or overcast day.

Once you are in the center of the crater bowl, the circular rim above looks much the same all the way around its circumference. A compass is an absolute must to keep you from getting confused and going out the wrong direction.

The approach to the crater can be made from either the East Crater Trail No. 48 from the east or the Pacific Crest National Scenic Trail No. 2000 from the west. I recommend the Crest Trail because its new location (1975) traverses north to south around the west side of the crater and part way up its side. This route will bring you within about 0.3 mile below the crater rim and eliminate the longer cross country hike required from an east side approach.

Hike south from Junction Lake on the Crest Trail for about one mile. Look up to your left (east) and you will see the crater rim above. Set your compass course and start climbing. Take it slow and easy because you will be chugging upward about 400 feet in 0.3 mile.

If you do not feel confident with a compass, bring along strips of colored, plastic surveyors' tape and attach them to tree limbs about 100 feet apart. These strips will direct you back to the trail on your return trip. Be sure to retrieve the tape strips on your way out.

The crater bowl is eerie but beautiful. A treeless meadow and a tarn are in its center, and to stand there looking up at its outer rim gives the feeling of being in a prehistoric world. You do not expect to see dinosaurs, but you are aware of bears, cougars and wildcats because their signs are all around, at least they were during my 1976 trip. The thought might even cross your mind that this is a logical place for Bigfoot to live.

A hiking partner once remarked, "If I wanted to locate a place where no one would ever find me, here is where I would come."

East Crater is awesome, not recommended for those who suffer from claustrophobia or for those who would rather avoid extremely lonely and mysterious places.

A single day trip into the East Crater and back to your car involves about eight miles of strenuous hiking. Your elevation gain will be 1,200 feet. You had better allow a full day for this one.

GIFFORD PEAK WAY (TRAIL)

Seven scenic lakes and several colorful meadows are located along this trail which parallels Falls Creek to its headwater source. You can take a short 1½ mile jaunt into these lakes and meadows or continue on for an approximate eight mile loop trip via the Pacific Crest National Scenic Trail and the Indian Race Track trails. The path is a lonely one, but may lead to unexpected excitement. (See chapter on *Big Foot Territory*.)

Drive north from Carson to Road N605. Follow N605 all the way to the "Indian Race Track No. 171" trail sign just north of Falls Creek. Driving distance from Carson is 21.2 miles.

From Trout Lake, drive west on Road 123, then N60 to the intersection with Road N605. Turn north (right) on N605 to the trail sign. Driving distance from Trout Lake is approximately 24 miles.

Gifford Peak Way Trail has an interesting history. The trail existed as early as 1922. A Columbia National Forest map for that year shows it proceeding northeasterly through the seven lakes, continuing northerly to the west of Gifford Peak and intersecting the old Crest Trail (now Trail 111) near the Umtux lakes. Some say it was an old Indian trail later used by sheepmen to bring their flocks to the high meadows. 1940 was the last year the trail appeared on the maps, so it was probably abandoned around the time the Columbia National Forest became the Gifford Pinchot National Forest in 1949. Back in those days trails were called "ways."

At one time, a trail was built extending easterly from the lakes and connecting with the old Crest Trail over a saddle between Gifford Peak and Berry Mountain. None of the old maps show this trail although it is visible today as if saved by time. This trail extension is the one you will follow on the eight mile loop hike.

Dedicated private citizens have kept the trail open as far as the lakes and it is in better condition than some of the other Indian Heaven trails. It is hoped that the Forest Service will bring it back into their trail inventory.

To locate the trail head, hike 0.2 mile on the Indian Race Track Trail No. 171 and look to your left (north) for the trail fork. The fork is located within hearing distance of Falls Creek, but an estimated 350 feet short. Do not be confused by another fork at about the same location, but on the opposite (right) side of the trail. This one will take you back to the road south of your car.

The trail commences at an elevation of approximately 3,600 feet. It ascends rapidly through the forest in a northeasterly direction for about 0.5 mile. Here it levels out and proceeds through small meadows for another 0.5 mile. The ground cover is now bear grass (squaw) and huckleberry brush with wild flowers blooming in late July and August.

The path starts to climb again for another 0.3 mile and continues with a gentle ascent for 0.2 mile to the Darlene Lakes.

Keep your eyes out for old Columbia National Forest markers on trees. These small metal signs could date back over 50 years. I recall one which read "Falls Creek Basin."

Darlene Lakes is a name used to generally define seven small lakes situated at approximately 4,200 feet. All are in close proximity, but the trail touches only one. You must look to the left and right of the trail for openings in the trees, then move in the direction of the opening to discover the lake. Three of the lakes have names: Janet, Peggy and Darlene. Darlene is the eastern lake of the group, being 2.0 acres in area and 15 feet deep. Peggy is the western, is 2.5 acres in area and 10 plus feet deep. Janet lies about 800 feet east from Peggy, is 2.0 acres in area and 25 feet deep.

It was not until recent years that these lakes were named. A friend, now retired from the Forest Service, informed me that the lakes were named after Forest Service employees' wives. He also stated, "This is against the law. You cannot name a lake after a living person." Be that as it may, the lakes are little gems and you will enjoy visiting all seven of them.

Your return to the car will be mostly downhill, completing a round trip hike of approximately three miles. Your elevation gain, 700 feet. (U.S. Geological Survey, Wind River, Washington.)

You should allow at least three hours for the hike as it will take extra time to locate all of the lakes.

To make the eight mile loop hike, continue easterly beyond the lakes. The trail becomes cluttered with downed timber, but can be followed. A compass is advisable, but it would be hard to get lost even without one.

The Pacific Crest National Scenic Trail proceeds south to north on top of the ridge, so just keep climbing until you intercept it. The trail distance from the lakes is about 0.5 mile and the elevation gain a tough 400 feet.

Turn south (right) on the Crest Trail and follow over Berry Mountain, then west on Trail 171A (shortcut) to the Indian Race Track, then northwest on Trail 171 (Indian Race Track) to your car. Allow a full day to complete this hike.

I am reluctant to hike the Gifford Peak Way Trail without a companion and without a side arm because of something up there around the Darlene Lakes.

In early December, 1976, I traversed the trail with Spencer Frey of Trout Lake. Near one lake we heard the crackling of brush in the trees surrounding a meadow. Near a second lake we heard a growling roar not more than 300 feet away. The terrifying sound was quite foreign from that made by a known animal.

Whatever it was stayed out of sight, following us from one lake to another.

THE PACIFIC CREST NATIONAL SCENIC TRAIL NO. 2000

The Pacific Crest Trail system extends from Canada to Mexico passing through the states of Washington, Oregon and California. It is approximately 2,400 miles in length and is located, for the most part, at a high elevation.

The part of the trail that traverses Indian Heaven follows the crest of the Cascade Mountains for approximately 17 miles through some of the most spectacular country you will ever see — a galaxy of lakes, mountains, craters and meadows.

Start the trip from the Crest Campground on Road N60 and hike north, or start from the Sawtooth huckleberry fields on Road 123 and hike south. I recommend the north to south route because of less climbing.

The trail head at the Sawtooth huckleberry fields can be reached from Carson by driving north on the Wind River Highway, then northeast on Road N73 to the end of the pavement. Angle right and continue on Road N73 to Road 123. Turn south (right) on Road 123 for 0.5 mile to the trail head. The driving distance from Carson is 34.5 miles. The trail head also may be reached in approximately 21.5 miles from Trout Lake by taking Road 123.

In recent years the Crest Trail has been relocated through Indian Heaven. Some of the relocation is an improvement because the new trail traverses mountain slopes and ridges which allow panoramic views. Other relocations are disappointing because the new trail bypasses some of the lakes and meadows. A combination route is suggested using both the new and the old trail to provide the most scenic enjoyment.

The trail commences southwesterly through the Sawtooth huckleberry fields. These fields comprise some 2,500 acres and are possibly the largest huckleberry fields in the world. The huckleberries on the east side of Road 123 are reserved for the exclusive use of the Indians.

Trees are sparse through the huckleberry fields, but increase in number as the path gains elevation. Noble fir, mountain hemlock and white pine soon join together in a "symphony in symmetry."

Choice of Trails

In about 0.8 mile the trail forks in two directions, giving a choice of routes to travel. The left fork (old trail) moves to the top of 5,369 foot Sawtooth Mountain, while the right fork (new trail), circumvents the mountain. I recommend the left fork (old trail) because the views from the top of the mountain are phenomenal including Mt. Rainier, the Goat Rocks, Mt. Adams, Sleeping Beauty, Mt. St. Helens, Lone Butte, Mt. Hood, plus the huckleberry fields and the Surprise Lakes.

The trail ascends the mountain and approaches the summit on the west side. Leave the trail and climb 100 feet to the top between the stone teeth of old Sawtooth. The drop-off on the southeast side of the mountain is terrifying. Look for herds of elk on the lower slopes.

From the summit the red and gray cindered trail switchbacks down the mountain to yet another trail fork.

Choice of Trails

The right fork is the old trail, the left fork the new. By all means, take the left fork (new) because the trail runs the east ridge of the saddle between Sawtooth Mountain and Bird Mountain, providing continuous views of the many peaks seen from the Sawtooth Mountain summit.

The path moves south to within a few hundred feet of the Cultus Creek Trail No. 108, then loops northwest, then south to the intersection with Trail 108. Travel distance to this intersection is approximately 3.9 miles.

Continue south from the Trail 108 intersection for 0.3 mile to the Wood Lake Trail No. 185. Take the 0.5 mile side trail for a view of one of the prettiest lakes in this part of Indian Heaven. Enjoy a efreshing swim or cast a line for brook trout.

Choice of Trails

The new and the old crest trails split at the Wood Lake Junction, both moving southerly on a relatively parallel course. The new trail avoids the small meadows and tarns, moves between Clear Lake and Deer Lake (cross country side trips), crosses Trail 33 at Bear Lake (2.5 miles), and arrives at Junction Lake in another 1.7 miles. Altogether, a somewhat monotonous trip through the forest.

The old trail passes through or near meadows, alongside lakes, and is more interesting and scenic than the new trail.

Take the right fork at the Wood Lake Junction and follow the Old Crest Trail south for 0.3 mile to a junction with the north fork of Trail 29, then another 0.4 mile to a junction with the south fork of Trail 29, then 1.1 miles to Deer Lake.

Deer Lake lies about 100 yards left (east) of the trail, so look for an opening in the trees and for a side path in to the lake. A nice camping spot is located on a flat near the shore. The lake is situated at an elevation of 4,800 feet, is 5.5 acres in size and holds both brook and cutthroat trout.

The trail continues south past a side trail to the new Crest Trail in 0.3 mile and a side trail to Elk Lake in another 0.1 mile.

The Elk Lake side trail is 0.2 mile long. Watch for the sign on a tree on the right side of the trail. Elk Lake is 13 acres in area, over 17 feet deep and contains both brook and cutthroat trout. It lies at an elevation of 4,685 feet.

In 0.1 mile from the Elk Lake Trail junction, the path arrives at the northwest end of Bear Lake. Situated at 4,750 feet, Bear Lake is six acres in area, more than 32 feet deep and contains both brook and cutthroat trout. An obvious campsite is located just off the trail near the lake. Other sites are located farther south on the western shore and on a peninsula extending from the eastern shore.

The trail continues southeast, from Bear Lake, arriving at the intersection with the Indian Heaven Trail No. 33 in 0.4 mile and Acker Lake in another 0.1 mile.

Acker Lake marks the entry into the meadow park lands of Indian Heaven. Mountain heather and wild flowers carpet the area during their blooming season. The lake, named after George Acker of Carson, lies at an elevation of 4,650 feet and is 1.5 acre in area. It is

not stocked with fish. Do not confuse Acker Lake with a nameles
lake located directly across the trail to the left (east).

From Acker Lake the trail continues south, crosses Rush Creek, anc
arrives in 0.6 mile at the combined junction of the Chenamus Lake
Trail No. 29A and the **original** Pacific Crest Trail to Rock Lake
There are no signs at this junction, but you will observe paintec
guide posts for those trails through the meadow.*

The vast park lands to the west of this junction contain dozens of
small lakes. You could spend several days exploring the country. I
like to compass my way from one lake to another using the Lone
Butte, Washington, U.S. Geological Survey map.

In 1976 I flew the area with Hugh Ackroyd, prominent Portland,
Oregon, photographer. He commented, "Those park lands appear
more impressive than Oregon's Jefferson Park."

From the trail junction the path continues south, then southeast
0.5 mile to rejoin the new Crest Trail at Junction Lake. Junction
Lake is situated at an elevation of 4,730 feet and is eight acres in
area. It is another lake without fish. Good campsites are located at
the northwest end where the sandy shored lake makes a long, narrow
extension into the meadow.

Now follow the new crest trail south around the west end of the lake
for about 0.1 mile to the junction with the East Crater Trail No. 48.

Choice of Trails

The new Pacific Crest Trail moves south around the western slope of
East Crater. This is the route to take if you plan to hike in and out of
the crater. (See *East Crater Trail No. 48.*) Otherwise, the 1.9 mile
path to Blue Lake is an uneventful hike through the forest with
distant views of Lake Toke-Tie (pretty) and two other unnamed
lakes.

The Old Crest Trail wanders through meadow park lands and alongside Lake Sahalee-Tyee and Blue Lake. I recommend this route.

The path departs from the new Crest Trail and moves southwesterly
at a right angle. You will find the fork about opposite the intersection with the East Crater Trail No. 48.

Now proceed down into the meadow park land and follow for

*The Forest Service may remove guide posts from abandoned trails. If the posts
are missing, hikers must look for the trail commencement at the meadow's
edge.

approximately 0.9 mile to the intersection with the Thomas Lake Trail No. 111. Turn left (southeast) and follow for approximately 0.3 mile to Lake Sahalee-Tyee (great spirit).

Because of its round appearance, Lake Sahalee-Tyee is thought to lie in the bowl of an extinct volcanic crater. It is situated at an elevation of 4,700 feet, is seven acres in area, over 25 feet deep and contains both brook and cutthroat trout. A near level campsite is located near the western shore about 50 feet from the trail. In the past the lake has been called other names such as Round Lake, Indian Heaven Lake and Green Lake.

From Lake Sahalee-Tyee the trail moves southeast, parallels Blue Lake along its eastern shore to the intersection with the Pacific Crest Trail in 0.2 mile, then follows the new trail south to the intersection with the Tombstone Lake Trail No. 55 in about 0.1 mile.

Blue Lake lies at an elevation of 4,640 feet, is 12 acres in area, 46 plus feet deep and holds both brook and cutthroat trout. The rich color of the water rivals that of Oregon's Crater Lake. A small campsite is located on the east side near the trail, but the main camp area is located at the southeast end of the lake where there is space for about ten camps. Another site is situated on a small peninsula which extends into the lake west of the main camp.

Choice of Trails

The Old Crest Trail (now signed "Tombstone Lake Trail No. 55") proceeds southeast past Tombstone Lake (0.2 mile), spring camp (another 1.8 miles), and rejoins the Pacific Crest Trail just north of the "Short Cut Trail No. 171A" in another 1.6 miles. This route is easier hiking than Trail 2000, but lacking in scenic highlights; the principal point of interest being a huge rock projecting from the water of Tombstone Lake which resembles a tombstone you might see in an old church cemetery. Take the 0.4 mile side (round) trip into Tombstone Lake if you have the time.

The new Crest Trail allows dozens of inspiring views, and is the one you should take. Bypass the Old Crest Trail (Tombstone Lake Trail No. 55) and climb the New Crest Trail southwesterly up to the saddle between Gifford Peak (5,368 feet) and Berry Mountain (4,987 feet). Now follow south along the ridge and enjoy the parade of views: Gifford Peak is to the north, Lemei Rock and Mt. Adams to the northeast, Sleeping Beauty to the east, Mt. St. Helens to the northwest, and Red Mountain and Mt. Hood to the south. At one point you can observe the Wind River drainage area on the west (right) side of the trail and the White Salmon River drainage area on the east (left) side of the trail.

Now climb near the top of Berry Mountain, then switch back down the cindered slopes to the intersection with the Short Cut Trail No 171A. The travel distance from Blue Lake to this intersection i approximately 4.1 miles.

Trail Choice to Your Shuttle Car

The Crest Trail continues south past Green Lake (0.5 mile) and Sheep Lakes (0.8 mile) to Road N60 and Crest Camp (another 1.7 miles). The trail is mostly downhill but lacking in scenic highlights

The Short Cut Trail No. 179A leads west to the Indian Race Track then south on Trail 179 to Road N538 near the top of Red Mountain. This is the route I recommend.

Leave the Crest Trail and follow Trail 179A west (right) to the Indian Race Track in 0.5 mile. The near level path will lead directly onto the east end of the Race Track.

Now turn left (south) and follow Trail 179 for 0.8 mile to Road N538 near the top of the mountain. Climb up the old fire lookout for a view of five snow-capped giants.

The trail route I have recommended is approximately 15.5 miles in length; 16.5 miles with side trips into Wood Lake and Elk Lake.

The new Pacific Crest Trail is approximately 16.7 miles long; 18.1 miles with side trips into Wood Lake and Elk Lake.

Regardless of which route you take, allow a minimum of two days with overnight camping. Three days would be better.

When you have concluded this scenic adventure through Indian Heaven, I am sure you will understand the exclamation of one of my companions who had just completed the jaunt, "That was the trip of a lifetime!"

SEMI-LOOP TRAILS

The following semi-loop trails, short and long, have been included to show visitors the most scenic areas in the interior of Indian Heaven. They have been planned to give a good sampling of lakes, meadows, craters and mountains which can be enjoyed along or just off the trails.

THOMAS LAKE TRAIL NO. 111 (Short Loop)

The first 2.1 miles of this hike are described in trail Chapter 2 *Thomas Lake Trail No. 111.* For driving directions to the trail head, see page 39.

The loop portion of this trip commences at Rock Lake. Look for the old trail sign as you approach the lake. Turn north (left) at the sign and proceed through a large meadow. The path is indistinct, so be careful to follow the painted "guide posts" in order to pick up the path extension at the north edge of the meadow.

The path drops abruptly for the first 0.3 mile and enters some of the prettiest park land in Indian Heaven. Why the trail was removed from Forest Service inventory remains a mystery.

In about one mile the path proceeds across what is known as the

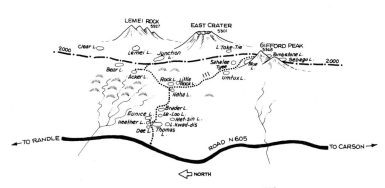

THOMAS LAKE TRAIL NO. 111
(SHORT LOOP)

"Indian Heaven Grand Meadow." This part of the trail can be trick because travelers tend to disperse through the meadow and a distinc path has never been established. Follow the guide posts, being carefu not to confuse them with nearby posts directing travelers from th Chenamus Lake Trail No. 29A. Both trails converge like the point o a triangle and intersect, together, at the Old Crest Trail (relocated i 1977).

As described in Chapter 7 *Chenamus Lake Trail No. 29A*, som thoughtful person erected a dead tree limb, with a white clotl attached to its top, at the point of the trail intersection. If it is stil there, head directly for it.

Now turn southeast (right) and follow the old Crest Trail for 0.' mile to Junction Lake. Pick up the Pacific Crest National Scenic Trai No. 2000 and follow south for two miles around the base of Eas Crater to Blue Lake.

In about a mile from Junction Lake look above you (east) to observ the East Crater rim. Hike cross country over the rim and into th bowl if you have the time and inclination for the side trip.

The trail moves beyond East Crater with several lakes appearing t the left (southeast) below the trail. The first one is called Lak Toke-Tie, meaning pretty. The others are unnamed. Cross countr travel is required to reach them.

The path arrives at the intersection with the Thomas Lake Trail No 111 at the southeast end of Blue Lake. Turn northwest (right) and hike back to your car in 3.3 miles.

Total travel distance for this trip is approximately nine miles. A overnight camping trip is recommended for a more leisurely enjoy ment of the trail, but you can hike it in less than a day if you keer moving.

THOMAS LAKE TRAIL NO. 111 (Long Loop)

The first 3.1 miles of this trip are identical to the short loop de scribed above. The route changes at the "Indian Heaven Granc Meadow" intersection with the old Crest Trail and proceeds nortl (left) instead of south as described in the short loop.

Follow the old Crest Trail for 0.7 mile past Acker Lake to its junc tion with the Indian Heaven Trail No. 33. Turn northeast (right) or the Indian Heaven Trail and continue for approximately 0.3 mile to

78

Bear Lake. Cross over the Pacific Crest National Scenic Trail No. 2000 near the southeast end of Bear Lake and continue on the Indian Heaven Trail to Clear Lake (0.3 mile), the northeast end of Clear Lake (0.5 mile) and the intersection with the Lemei Lake Trail No. 179 (0.1 mile). Turn southeast (right) on the Lemei Lake Trail and follow the guide posts through a huge meadow.

The Lemei Lake Trail section of the trip is pure delight. The country is so typical of the high, interior, plateau of Indian Heaven, with meadows interspersed with alpine trees and abundant wild flowers blooming in their season.

Watching carefully, you will observe an old Columbia National Forest sign on a tree which reads "Lemei Lane." These trails were called "ways" and also "lanes" in the early 1900's.

Lemei Lake is 0.5 mile from the Indian Heaven Trail intersection. It is situated at an elevation of 5,000 feet and is seven acres in size. Look for eternal ice in a shaded area alongside the trail just south of the lake. The Indian word, Lemei, means "The Old Lady."

From Lemei Lake the trail bends southwesterly, crosses Rush Creek in 0.8 mile and arrives at Junction Lake in another 0.5 mile. From Junction Lake, hike south on the Pacific Crest National Scenic Trail No. 2000 to Blue Lake (2 miles), then northwest and west on the Thomas Lake Trail No. 111 back to your car (3.3 miles).

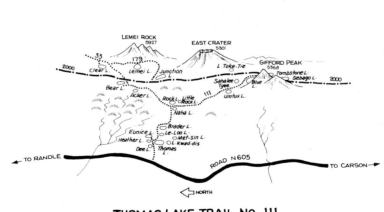

THOMAS LAKE TRAIL NO. 111
(LONG LOOP)

Total travel distance for this trip is approximately 12 miles. Plan two days with an overnight camp to enjoy this one.

INDIAN HEAVEN TRAIL NO. 33 (Short Loop)

The first 2.3 miles of this hike were described in trail Chapter 4 *Indian Heaven Trail No. 33 (Sahalee-Tyee).* Driving directions to the trail head at Cultus Creek Campground are on page 52.

The loop portion of this trip commences at the intersection of the Indian Heaven Trail with the Lemei Lake Trail No. 179. (Do not confuse with the Lemei Trail No. 34.)

Turn southeast (left) on the Lemei Lake Trail and follow the guide posts through a huge meadow, then park lands, to Lemei Lake in 0.5 mile. From Lemei Lake the trail moves southwesterly, crosses Rush Creek in 0.8 mile and arrives at Junction Lake in another 0.5 mile. Hike just beyond the new Pacific Crest Trail No. 2000 and look for the old Crest Trail which takes off northwesterly at a right angle. Drop down into the Indian Heaven "grand meadow" and follow the old trail north past Acker Lake to the Indian Heaven Trail intersection in 1.2 miles. Turn right on the Indian Heaven Trail (just beyond Acker Lake) and follow its full 3.6 mile length back to your car at Cultus Creek Campground.

Total travel distance for this trip is approximately 8.9 miles. You can

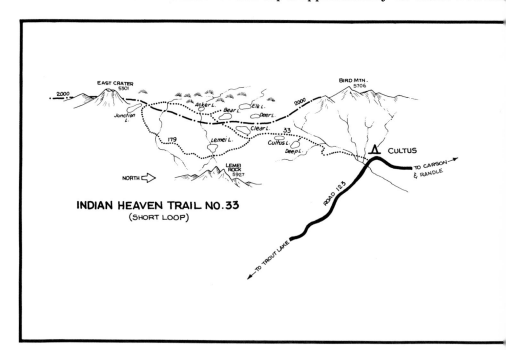

INDIAN HEAVEN TRAIL NO. 33
(SHORT LOOP)

ike it in less than a day, but you should plan two days with an
overnight camping trip because there is so much to see, and because
there are tempting side trips you may want to take.

NDIAN HEAVEN TRAIL NO. 33 (Long Loop)

The preceding short loop description covers the first 4.1 miles of this
trip. The route changes at Junction Lake and proceeds south (left)
on the Pacific Crest National Scenic Trail No. 2000.

Follow the Crest Trail south to Blue Lake in two miles. Turn northwest (right) on the Thomas Lake Trail No. 111 past Lake Sahalee-
Tyee in 0.2 mile, the old Crest Trail Junction in another 0.3 mile,
and arrive at Rock Lake in another 0.7 mile. Continue north (straight
ahead) from Rock Lake and follow the **original** Crest Trail for about
one mile to the old Crest Trail intersection at the Indian Heaven
"grand meadow." Turn north (left) on the old Crest Trail to its
ntersection with the Indian Heaven Trail No. 33 in 0.7 mile. Turn
northeast (right) on the Indian Heaven Trail and follow for 3.6 miles
back to your car at the Cultus Creek Campground.*

Total travel distance for this trip is approximately 12.6 miles. Plan
two days with an overnight camping trip.

*The Forest Service may remove guide posts from abandoned trails. If the posts
are missing, hikers must look for the trail commencement at the meadow's
edge.

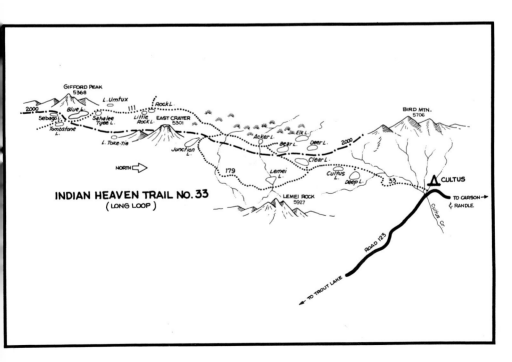

INDIAN HEAVEN TRAIL NO. 33
(LONG LOOP)

This route will pass alongside a dozen lakes and through several mile of meadow park land that are truly representative of the India Heaven interior.

LEMEI TRAIL NO. 34 (Short Loop)

The first 5.4 miles of this hike are described in trail Chapter 3 *Leme Trail No. 34*. Driving directions to the trail head at the Little Goose Campground are on page 46.

The loop portion of this trip commences at Cultus Lake where Trai 34 intersects with the Indian Heaven Trail No. 33.

Turn left (southwest) on Trail 33 and hike approximately 0.3 mile to the intersection with the Lemei Lake Trail No. 179. Turn left (south east) on the Lemei Lake Trail to Lemei Lake (0.5 mile) and Junction Lake in another 1.3 miles. Hike just beyond the Pacific Crest Na tional Scenic Trail No. 2000 and look for the old Crest Trail which takes off northwesterly at a right angle. Drop down into the Indian Heaven "grand meadow" and follow the old Crest Trail north past Acker Lake to the Indian Heaven Trail intersection in 1.2 miles. Turn right (northeast) on the Indian Heaven Trail and follow approxi mately 1.3 miles back to the intersection with Lemei Trail No. 34 at Cultus Lake. Turn right (southeast) on the Lemei Trail. The return to your car is 5.1 miles.

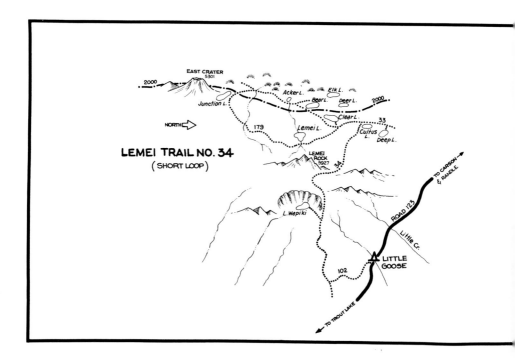

Total travel distance for this trip is approximately 15 miles. Two full days with overnight camping is recommended.

LEMEI TRAIL NO. 34 (Long Loop)

The first 7.5 miles of this trip are identical to the short loop. The route changes at Junction Lake where the Lemei Trail No. 179 intersects the Pacific Crest National Scenic Trail No. 2000.

Turn left (south) on the Pacific Crest National Scenic Trail and hike two miles to Blue Lake. Turn right (northwest) on the Thomas Lake Trail No. 111 past Lake Sahalee-Tyee in 0.2 mile, the old Crest Trail Junction in another 0.3 mile, and arrive at Rock Lake in another 0.7 mile. Continue north (straight ahead) from Rock Lake and follow the **original** Crest Trail for about one mile to the old Crest Trail intersection at the Indian Heaven "grand meadow." Turn north (left) on the old Crest Trail to its intersection with the Indian Heaven Trail No. 33 in 0.7 mile. Turn northeast (right) on the Indian Heaven Trail (just beyond Acker Lake) and follow approximately 1.3 miles back to the intersection with the Lemei Trail No. 34 at Cultus Lake. Turn southeast (right) on the Lemei Trail. The return to your car is 5.1 miles.

Total travel distance for this trip is approximately 18.8 miles. Two full days with overnight camping is recommended.

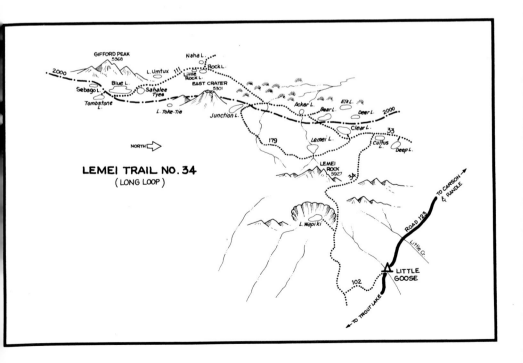

LEMEI TRAIL NO. 34
(LONG LOOP)

EAST CRATER TRAIL NO. 48 (Short Loop)

The first 2.5 miles of this hike are described in trail Chapter 8 *East Crater Trail No. 48*. Driving directions to the trail head are on page 66.

The loop portion of this trip commences at the intersection of the East Crater Trail with the Pacific Crest National Scenic Trail No. 2000 at Junction Lake. Turn north (right) on the Pacific Crest Trail, cross a foot bridge and start looking for the old Crest Trail which proceeds northwesterly (left) away from the Pacific Crest Trail. Follow the old Crest Trail down into the Indian Heaven "grand meadow," then northward past Acker Lake, arriving at the intersection with the Indian Heaven Trail No. 33 in 1.2 miles. Turn northeast on the Indian Heaven Trail and continue for approximately 0.3 mile to Bear Lake. Cross over the Pacific Crest National Scenic Trail No. 2000 near the southeast end of Bear Lake and continue northeast on the Indian Heaven Trail to Clear Lake (0.3 mile), the northeast end of Clear Lake (0.5 mile), and the intersection with the Lemei Lake Trail No. 179 (0.1 mile). Turn right (southeast) on the Lemei Lake Trail to Lemei Lake (0.5 mile) and Junction Lake in another 1.3 miles. Pick up the East Crater Trail No. 48 and the return to your car will be 2.5 miles.

Total travel distance is approximately 9.2 miles. You can hike it in a day, but I have never found any fun in a hurried trip. Better take two days with an overnight camp.

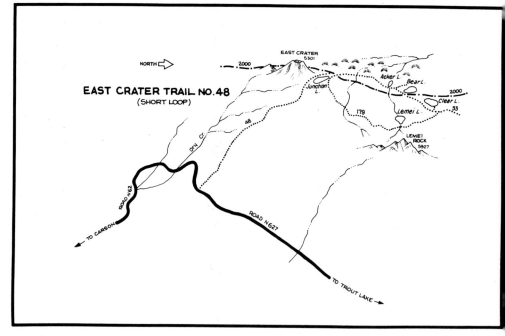

EAST CRATER TRAIL NO. 48 (Long Loop)

The long loop commences at Junction Lake the same as the short loop. In this case, however, the route is south (left) on the Pacific Crest National Scenic Trail No. 2000 instead of northwest on the old Crest Trail.

Follow the Pacific Crest Trail south from Junction Lake to Blue Lake for two miles. Turn northwest (right) on the Thomas Lake Trail No. 111 to Rock Lake in 1.2 miles. Continue north (straight ahead) from Rock Lake and follow the **original** Crest Trail for about one mile to the old Crest Trail intersection at the Indian Heaven "grand meadow." Turn north (left) on the old Crest Trail to its intersection with the Indian Heaven Trail No. 33 (0.7 mile). Turn northeast (right) on the Indian Heaven Trail (just beyond Acker Lake) and follow for approximately 0.3 mile to Bear Lake. Cross over the Pacific Crest National Scenic Trail No. 2000 near the southeast end of Bear Lake and continue northeast on the Indian Heaven Trail to Clear Lake (0.3 mile), the northeast end of Clear Lake (0.5 mile), and the intersection with the Lemei Lake Trail No. 179 (0.1 mile). Turn right (southeast) on the Lemei Lake Trail to Lemei Lake (0.5 mile) and Junction Lake, another 1.3 miles. Pick up the East Crater Trail No. 48 and return to your car (2.5 miles).

Total travel distance is approximately 12.9 miles. This is a long, tough hike. Allow two full days with overnight camping.

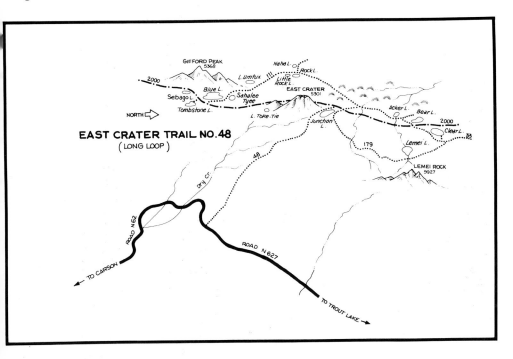

CHENAMUS LAKE TRAIL NO. 29A (Short Loop)

The first 3.5 miles of this hike are described in trail Chapter 7 *Chenamus Lake Trail No. 29A.* For driving directions to the starting point at the trail head of the Placid Lake Trail No. 29, see page 63.

The loop portion of this trip commences at the very end of the Chenamus Lake Trail where it intersects the old Crest Trail at the Indian Heaven "grand meadow."

Turn north (left) on the old Crest Trail and follow past Acker Lake to the junction with the Indian Heaven Trail No. 33 (0.7 mile). Turn northeast (right) on the Indian Heaven Trail and continue for approximately 0.3 mile to Bear Lake. Cross over the Pacific Crest National Scenic Trail No. 2000 near the southeast end of Bear Lake and continue on the Indian Heaven Trail to Clear Lake (0.3 mile), the northeast end of Clear Lake (0.5 mile), and the intersection with the Lemei Lake Trail No. 179 (0.1 mile). Turn southeast (right) on the Lemei Lake Trail to Lemei Lake (0.5 mile) and Junction Lake in another 1.3 miles. Hike just beyond the Pacific Crest National Scenic Trail No. 2000 and look for the old Crest Trail which takes off northwesterly at a right angle. Drop down into the Indian Heaven "grand meadow" and follow the old Crest Trail for 0.5 mile to its intersection with the Chenamus Lake Trail No. 29A. Turn northwest (left) on the Chenamus Lake Trail being careful to follow the guideposts across the meadow in a northwesterly direction. The guideposts going southwesterly will head you toward Rock Lake. Pick up the

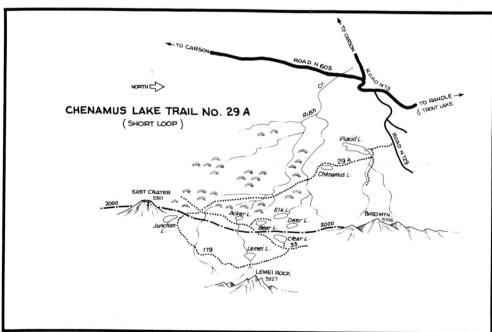

trail at meadow's end and return to your car (3.5 miles).

Total travel distance for this trip is approximately 11.2 miles. Allow two days with overnight camping.

CHENAMUS LAKE TRAIL NO. 29A (Long Loop)

The first 4.2 miles of this trip are identical to the foregoing short loop. The route changes at Junction Lake and turns south on the Pacific Crest National Scenic Trail No. 2000 instead of northwesterly on the old Crest Trail, short loop.

Pick up the Pacific Crest National Scenic Trail No. 2000 at the northwest end of Junction Lake. Turn south (left) and follow two miles to Blue Lake. Turn northwest (right) on the Thomas Lake Trail No. 111 to Rock Lake in 1.2 miles. Continue north (straight ahead) from Rock Lake and follow the **original** Crest Trail for about one mile to the old Crest Trail intersection at the Indian Heaven meadow.

This trail intersection is also the intersection of the Chenamus Lake Trail No. 29A which you will follow on the return trip to your car. At this point, be sure to turn back at the old Crest Trail intersection and follow the guideposts **northwesterly** to pick up the trail at the end of the meadow and hike home in 3.5 miles.

Total travel distance is approximately 14.8 long miles. Plan two days with overnight camping.

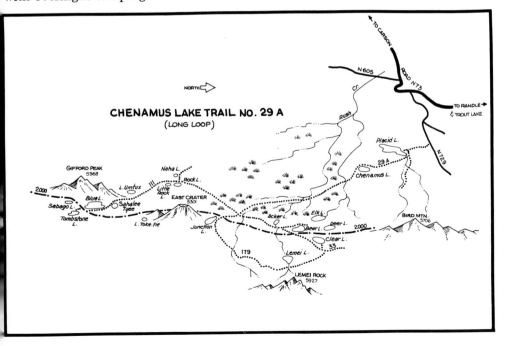

FULL LOOP TRAILS

The following full loop trails differ from the semi-loop trails in that no retracing of any part of the trail more than one-half mile is required to complete the loop back to the point of origin.

LOOP TRAIL NO. 1

Loop Trail No. 1 originates at the trail head of the "Placid Lake Trail No. 29." For driving directions to the trail head, see page 60.

Hike 0.5 mile to Placid Lake. Turn southeasterly (left) just short of the lake and proceed 0.1 mile to the Chenamus Lake Trail No. 29A. Turn south (right) on the Chenamus Lake Trail and follow 3 miles to the intersection with the **old** Crest Trail at the **Indian Heaven grand meadow.** Turn north (left) on the old Crest Trail, bypassing Indian Heaven Trail No. 33, and follow for 2.6 miles to the intersection with the Placid Lake Trail No. 29. Turn northwest (left) and follow for two miles back to your car.

This trip takes you alongside Placid Lake, Chenamus Lake, Acker Lake, Bear Lake, Elk Lake (a 0.2 mile side trip), Deer Lake, and a number of unnamed lakes. You cross meadows as beautiful as you will ever see.

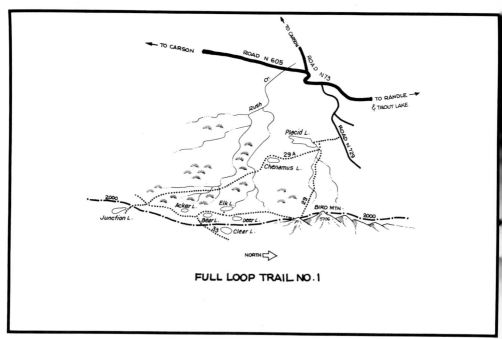

FULL LOOP TRAIL NO. 1

Total travel distance for this trip is approximately 8.2 miles; 8.6 miles with the Elk Lake side trip. You can hike it in a day, but if you want to enjoy it more, take two days with overnight camping.

LOOP TRAIL NO. 2

Loop Trail No. 2 originates at the trail head of the Indian Race Track Trail No. 171 at Falls Creek. Do not confuse it with the Red Mountain trail head. For driving directions, see the second approach to the race track, page 38.

Hike 0.2 mile on the Indian Race Track Trail No. 171. Turn northeast (left) on the unsigned Gifford Peak Way Trail and follow for approximately 1.5 miles to the Darlene Lakes. Continue easterly (straight ahead) for approximately 0.5 mile to the intersection with the Pacific Crest National Scenic Trail No. 2000 located on top of the ridge of a saddle between Gifford Peak and Berry Mountain. This steep section of the trail between the Darlene Lakes and the Crest Trail is followable, but a compass is needed unless very familiar with the trail. Should you lose the trail, keep climbing to the top of the ridge above you until you intercept the Crest Trail, but keep alert that you do not overstep it.

Turn south (right) on the Crest Trail and proceed for approximately three miles to the intersection with the Short-Cut Trail No. 171A.

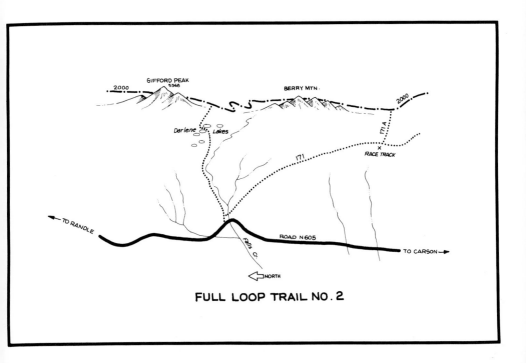

FULL LOOP TRAIL NO. 2

Turn west (right) on the Short-Cut Trail and hike 0.5 mile to the Indian Race Track. Turn northwest (right) around the east side of Race Track Lake and follow the Indian Race Track Trail No. 171 for 2.3 miles to your car.

The first part of the trail will bring you through the seven Darlene Lakes. The trail touches only one, so look for openings in the trees to discover the others. The Pacific Crest National Scenic Trail section of the trip will provide outstanding views of Lemei Rock, Mt. Adams, Sleeping Beauty and Mt. Hood. The Indian Race Track on Trail 171 will please you because of its historical significance.

Total travel distance for this trip is approximately eight miles, of which about one-half is tough going. Better take two days with overnight camping rather than overdo it.

LOOP TRAIL NO. 3

Loop Trail No. 3 originates at Cultus Creek Campground. For driving directions to the campground and to the Indian Heaven Trail No. 33 trail head, see page 52.

Hike the Indian Heaven Trail No. 33 for 3.2 miles to the Pacific Crest National Scenic Trail No. 2000 at Bear Lake. Turn north (right) on the Pacific Crest Trail and follow for 2.5 miles to the intersection with the Cultus Creek Trail No. 108 just north of the Wood Lake

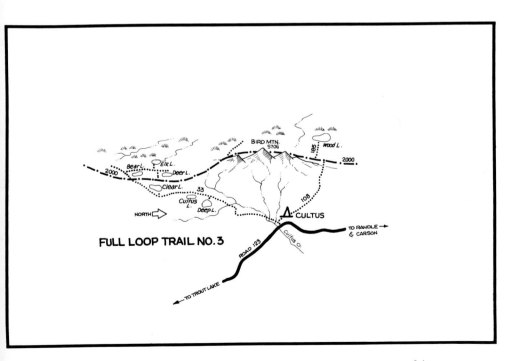

FULL LOOP TRAIL NO. 3

Trail No. 185 exit. Turn east (right) on Trail No. 108 and follow for 1.5 miles back to your car.

The Indian Heaven Trail No. 33 portion of this hike will take you by Deep Lake (a 0.2 mile side trail), Cultus Lake, Clear Lake, and several lovely meadows. The Pacific Crest National Scenic Trail No. 2000 portion of the hike will take you by Bear Lake, Elk Lake (a 0.4 mile side trail), Deer Lake (an estimated 0.1 mile cross country hike), and Wood Lake (a 0.5 mile side trail). The Cultus Creek Trail No. 108 will provide grandiose views of Sawtooth Mountain, the Goat Rocks and Mt. Adams.

The hike can be made in reverse by starting from the Cultus Creek Trail No. 108; however, I do not recommend it because of the severity of the 1.5 mile climb to the Pacific Crest Trail.

Total travel distance for this loop trip is approximately 7.2 miles, or 9.6 miles with side trips. You can hike it in less than a day, including side trips, but that is hurrying. Two days with an overnight camping trip would be more enjoyable.

Sawtooth Mountain

PART 3:

Information for the Indian Heaven Traveler

SPECIFIC INFORMATION

CAMPGROUNDS NEAR TRAIL HEADS

For those who wish to day-hike and return to camp in an established campground, Indian Heaven offers many opportunities. Two of the largest campgrounds are located at trail heads to Indian Heaven. Cultus Creek, with 66 tent sites, is the starting point for both Trail 33 and Trail 108, and Little Goose, with 36 tent sites, is the beginning point for Trail 102. Goose Lake Campground contains 27 tent sites plus eight trailer sites and is located just a few miles from the Red Mountain take-off of Trail 171 to the Indian Race Track. Goose Lake provides boating, swimming and fishing for eastern brook trout. Horses may be kept at Little Goose campground.

Other campgrounds in close proximity to Indian Heaven are Tillicum with 49 tent sites, Saddle with 16 sites, South with 9 sites, Smoky Creek with 3 sites and Peterson Prairie with 19 sites. Three small campgrounds are located near the Sawtooth berry fields and the Surprise Lakes. They are called Cold Spring, Meadow Creek and Surprise Lakes. Indians use these three camps during the berry picking season. All camps are well marked on the Gifford Pinchot National Forest map which is available at the Forest Supervisor Gifford Pinchot National Forest office in Vancouver, Washington (P.O. Box 449), or can be obtained in person from any of the district ranger stations or by mail from the following ranger stations: St. Helens, Cougar, Washington 98616; Mt. Adams, Trout Lake, Washington 98650; Packwood, Packwood, Washington 98361; Randle, Randle, Washington 98377 and Wind River, Carson, Washington 98610. The map costs 50¢.

There is an overnight camping charge at Tillicum, Cultus, Peterson Prairie and Goose Lake.

Reservations are not required, but you should observe "Notices" establishing limitations on the period of time you may camp in a given campground. The length of stay is generally limited to 14 days, but this is subject to change.

I suggest you ask for a free copy of *Camping Regulations* when ordering or picking up your map. Camping regulations have changed a lot in recent years. New requirements also cover such things as public behavior, audio devices and vehicles.

FISHING TECHNIQUES

Indian Heaven fishing is best from August until the end of the Washington State regulated season. The higher the lakes, the better the fishing gets, because for every 1,500 feet one climbs, summer is a month shorter, so fish have to hurry. At a mile above sea level the trout have less than half the time their low land relatives enjoy between spring breakup and winter freeze. So they rush spawning and then hurry to rebuild their muscles. Since they are running out of time, they are feeding at a fast tempo. They fall for imitation lures with gusto.

Before one gets carried away with the idea he will catch a fish with every cast, here are some suggestions on how to fish the Indian Heaven lakes. The lakes are clear and cold, so clear in fact that eight pound monofilament looks like cable. Fish will automatically shy away from large lures and lines. Try dense lures of the spoon variety to reach out without spreading pandemonium. A small Colorado or Mepps spinner with a speck of worm can be a murderous lure. Erratic spinner movement is important. Trout will rarely hit any spinner moving at a slow, even speed. Most popular patterns of flies, both wet and dry, will do the job. Best are brown, black and gray color ranges in mosquito, gnats, brown hackle and bivisible variations. Try to match the fly to the "hatch." Streamers can be effective just before dark. Spinfishers can use them with a small bubble. An imitation grasshopper can be effective, too. Grease a size 4 or 6 hopper, and skim it in short pulls across the surface. Usually fishing action disappears as morning shadows leave the lake. When afternoon shadows reappear, try the shady side of the lake. Explore near inlet streams, outlet streams, log jams, or dead trees protruding into the lake.

"Light weight" equipment is important. "Light weight" means one will be able to present tiny morsels that wary fish will take when normal lures and flies frighten them. In addition to attracting more fish, lighter lines mean heavier action. Two pound mono or a 6X Tippet turns a 12-inch trout into an exciting leviathan.

Rubber rafts are helpful in getting out to deep water, but unless coming on horseback, the high lake trails are difficult for the added pack weight. One can, however, bring rafts into some of the lower lakes. Placid Lake is just a half mile trail and it is only a three-quarter mile hike to Thomas, Dee, Heather and Eunice lakes.

PACK STRING

Fortunately, people who are not up to an Indian Heaven hiking trip can still enjoy the beauty and solitude, the great fishing and camping of high lonely places by letting a horse transport them up the trails. Trail riding requires no special training, and though pain will descend on muscles that have not been prepared for the saddle, tip-top physical condition is not required.

With horses carrying both you and your supplies, you can indulge in a lot of "at home" luxuries that you could not possibly carry in a backpack. Your layout can include tent, stove, pots, pans, plates, silverware, tons of food, coffee pot, dishpan, sleeping bags and camera equipment.

You can bring your own horses or go first class by hiring a packer and cook.

Spencer Frey, of Trout Lake, Washington, is the principal packer for the Indian Heaven back country as well as other nearby areas. He will supply everything except sleeping bags and your personal effects. He will also take you in, set up a "drop camp" and pick you up at a later date. He is an ex-Forest Service employee and is thoroughly familiar with the country.

Should you decide to pack-in with horses, you should read *Regulations of Travel and Recreation Livestock*, the U.S. Forest Service regulations affecting this form of travel.

1. Bringing or having any pack or saddle animal within 200 feet distance of the shoreline of any lake or stream except for the purpose of watering, loading or unloading, or through travel on an established trail is prohibited.

2. Loose herding of pack and saddle stock is prohibited on established routes; stock must be ridden or led.

3. Short cutting at trail switchbacks with horses or pack stock or on foot is prohibited.

4. Supplemental horse feed will be carried when camping overnight.

5. The size of group is limited to 20 people and/or livestock.

In addition to the above regulations, you will be required by law to have a shovel, ax and bucket to be used in case of uncontrolled fire.

I have observed considerable trail rutting on the forest approach trails caused by the compression of pack animals' hooves. Further trail erosion follows naturally when rain and snow melt flow down the sloping ruts. Much of this could be avoided if people would save their pack trip until September or October when the soil is usually dry.

The Forest Service is becoming increasingly concerned about the mpact of livestock on the scenic environment. An example of this concern is evidenced by a ruling affecting an area north of Mt. St. Helens and Spirit Lake. Horseriding activity in the Mt. Margaret back country is now limited to day use only.

f trail riders continue to ignore U.S. Forest Service regulations, a similar ruling, or a complete ban, could go into effect in Indian Heaven.

Horses, for some reason known only to them, will make a new trail alongside an existing trail. I have observed as many as three parallel trails. A rider should keep his horse on the main trail.

At campsites, horses should be tied well away from tent and cooking areas. Horse manure is not popular with hikers and campers. Keep in mind that violations of rules and lack of consideration for other campers could result in some drastic action affecting the use of pack animals in Indian Heaven.

CHINOOK

Among all the generations since 1811, Chinook Jargon has been used by upwards of a quarter of a million persons, to many of whom it was an everyday necessity. The jargon was widely used because it was a successful communication between persons of different tribes, nationalities and races. It was adopted and used by the traders, trappers, pioneers and early settlers.

Today you can have a lot of fun with a few Chinook words. Surprise and amuse your trail companions by referring to objects and things in Chinook. Here are a few of the words you will find most applicable to the Indian Heaven back country. You will be surprised to find how easy they are to remember once you start using them.

Black Bear	Chetwoot
Cougar	Hyas pusspuss
Elk	Moolack
Deer	Mowitch
Coyote	Talapus
Wildcat	Siwash pusspuss
Grey Wolf	Leloo
Beaver	Eena
Otter	Nenamooks
Muskrat	Emintepu
Squirrel	Kwiskwis
Skunk	Hummopoots
Flowers	Kloshe tupso
Meadow	Tupso Illalee

A canyon	Tanino
Valley	Kloshe Illalee
Mountain	Lamontay
Lake	Tsalil
A river	Chuck
A creek	Tenas chuck
A waterfall	Tumwata
Swift water	Skukum chuck
Trail	Ooahut
Sky	Koosah
Stars	Tsiltsil
The sun	Otelagh
Horse	Kuitan
Horseback	Kopa Kuitan
To gallop	Kwalal Kwalal
A bridle	Lableed
A saddle	Lasell
Saddle blanket	Lepishemo
Stirrup	Sitlay
Spur	Leseeblo
A whip	Lewhet
Corral	Kullah
A mosquito	Melakwa
Gnats	Dago
A wasp	Andialh
Flies	Lemosh
Insect sting	Keepwot
Angler	Pishman
A fish pole	Pishstick
A fishhook	Akik
A canoe	Canim
A paddle, an oar	Isick
Food	Muckamuck
Hungry	Olo
Thirsty	Ola, Kopachuck
A frying pan	Lapoel
Dishes	Leplah
Bowl or cup	Ooskan
A rifle	Calipeen
A bullet (arrow)	Kallitan
Knife	Opitsah
Axe	Lahash
Hatchet	Tenas Lahash
A shovel	Lapell
To pack	Lolo

Indian Baby on Croole Board

To swim	Sitshum
To climb	Klatawa Saghalie
To drink	Muckamuck Chuck
To row	Mamook Lalahm
Dawn	Cheechako light
Morning	Tenas sun
Noon	Sitkum sun
Afternoon	Kimtah Sitkum sun
Sunset	Klip sun
Night	Polaklie
Spring	Tenas Waum Illahee
Summer	Waum Illahee
Autumn	Tenas Cole Illahee
Winter	Cole Illahee
Kettle	Ketling
A bucket	Tamolitsh
Utensils	Ikta
Cook	Mamook piah Muckamuck
Basket	Opekwan
A small bird	Cheechee
The Bald Eagle	Chakchak
Woodpecker	Kokostick
Owl	Kwelkwel
Mallard Duck	Hahthaht
Raven, crow	Kahkah
Goose	Kalakala
Grouse	Siwash Lapool
Hawk	Shakshak
Blackbird	Pilokchok
Clothes	Iktas
Dress	Klootchman Coat
Pants	Sakoleks
Coat	Kapo
Shirt	Shut
Stocking	Stocken
Boots	stick shush
Berries	Olallie
Blackberries	Klale Olallie
Huckleberries	Shot Olallie
Salal berries	Salal Olallie

You will note the absence of the letter F in Chinook words. The Indians could not pronounce it. The word fish, for example, became pish.

From "Chinook: A History and Dictionary"
by Edward Thomas, Binford & Mort, Publishers, Portland

HEALTH, SAFETY, COMFORT AND SURVIVAL

Many excellent books have been written about health, safety, comfort and survival in the outdoors.

The intent of this chapter is for the inexperienced who are interested in Indian Heaven and will use this book as their reference.

Weather and Clothing

I shall always remember my first hike into the Indian Heaven back country. The chosen route was Trail 33 from the Cultus Creek Campground to the Pacific Crest National Scenic Trail No. 2000, which I would follow north to Trail 108 and back to the car. The air temperature was comfortable until I broke out of the trees into the high meadows between Deep Lake and Clear Lake. Here, under bright sunshine and clear blue skies, I became chilled, so much so that I had to keep moving to stay warm. I soon realized that the high elevation in combination with a cold east wind had created the temperature change. I was totally unprepared with inadequate clothing. I have since observed it is quite common for chilly east winds to accompany clear skies during late summer and fall.

The following wind chill factor chart will give you an idea of the effect of the wind at various speeds and different temperatures:

Wind speed Actual Temperature	10 mph	20 mph	30 mph
	What it equals in its effect on exposed flesh.		
55°	40°	32°	28°
40°	28°	18°	13°
30°	16°	4°	-2°
20°	4°	-10°	-18°
0°	-21°	-39°	-48°

On another hike into Rock Lake via the Thomas Lake Trail 111, the weather changed from morning clear skies to clouds to afternoon rain. This time I was prepared with adequate clothing to keep me warm, but with no hooded windbreaker to keep me dry.

Mountain weather is totally undependable, particularly on the western slopes of the Cascades. One should bring more clothes than he thinks he will need, clothes that may be added or taken off as required for comfort.

The following list is a guide to be used in preparing for a trip into the Indian Heaven back country:

FISH NET UNDERWEAR

SLACKS OR JEANS — (Wool is best. It dries quickly and, even when wet, will give some insulation from the cold.)

WOOL SHIRT

NYLON WEBBING BELT — (Does not dent your hips under a pack's waist belt.)

DOWN JACKET

HOODED, WATERPROOF WINDBREAKER

TWO PAIRS WOOL SOCKS — (One lightweight and tightly woven next to your feet, the other heavyweight over the first pair.)

LEATHER BOOTS — (Waterproofed with padded ankles and Vibram lug soles.)

Equipment
The Day Hike

BACK PACK

MATCHES — in waterproof container or a metal match.

KNIFE — to make kindling, for first aid and to clean fish.

CANDLE — to start a fire with wet wood.

SUNGLASSES — to protect your eyes from high altitude sun glare.

SMALL FLASHLIGHT — (Include extra penlight batteries and bulb.) If you are lost three flashes signal S.O.S.

CANTEEN — or plastic bottle.

LIGHTWEIGHT TROWEL — for sanitation.

COMPASS — I recommend one such as "Silva" that can be easily coordinated with a map.

TOILET TISSUE — Small Kleenex packs are less bulky.

THIS BOOK — for trail map, trail sketches and information.

U. S. GEOLOGICAL SURVEY TOPOGRAPHIC MAPS

THREE LARGE SAFETY PINS — Temporary repair of torn clothing, pack, etc.

MOLESKIN — for foot blisters and hot spots.

ALUMINUM FOIL — Signal mirror; form into a cup for drinking or pan for cooking or reflector oven.

MONOFILAMENT LINE — (10 ft. 25 pound test) Replace broken boot laces, tie splints to broken limbs, repair split seams in boots using heavy needle.

FIRST AID KIT — Add to kit items, aspirin and personal medications.

MOSQUITO REPELLENT

Equipment
The Combined Hiking and Camping Trip

You will need all the equipment listed above plus the following items:

SLEEPING BAG — Dacron or down filled.

MATTRESS — Ensolite or foam is more dependable than air filled rubber.

GROUND COVER — (10x8 foot plastic) Helps slow the transfer of body heat to the cold ground, helps keep your bag, your clothing, and your gear clean. Protects you from a rain shower when you pull the excess footage over your bag.

LIGHTWEIGHT, WATERPROOF TENT OR TARP — if you wish a roof over your head.

LIGHT NYLON CORD — to erect a tarp or cache food in a tree.

ALUMINUM MESS KIT — not necessary if you are using freeze-dried foods with their own serving pouch or tray. Just bring something to boil water in, a cup and a spoon.

SCOURING PAD WITH BUILT-IN SOAP — eliminates the need of an additional bar of soap.

PERSONAL ITEMS — toothbrush, comb, suntan lotion, etc., plus washcloth and towel.

BUTANE CARTRIDGE STOVE — an alternate to campfire cooking. It weighs about one pound eight ounces and burns 3 to 3½ hours per cartridge. Eliminates the hazard of gasoline. Butane can freeze in extremely cold weather (place the cartridge in your pocket or wrap in ensolite).

Food for a Day Hike

All you really need is "Gorp" and a canteen of water. What is "Gorp"? The common mixture calls for equal portions of raisins, peanuts and chocolate chips (regular brand M&M's work as well as chips). Some hikers mix in Granola with their Gorp.

Why Gorp? Because Gorp provides carbohydrates, proteins and fats that resupply the constant energy loss of the hiker. Carbohydrates (sweets) go almost instantly to the blood stream for quick energy. Fat produces longer lasting energy, and protein builds and bolsters muscle and other body tissue. At high altitudes, fats and proteins become increasingly hard to metabolize, but are still an important part of the diet.

Since a day hike does not require a heavy pack load, you may wish to take along other "hikers' favorites" such as pemmican, jerky, dried fruit, chocolate bars, fruit bars, or the old standby, "Kendal Mint Cake." One bar of the latter provides 600 calories. You might also bring a few salt tablets to take if sweating heavily, to ward off muscle cramps and dehydration. Hard candies are beneficial, too; they supply almost instant energy and help keep the mouth moist.

104

Food for the Combined
Hiking and Camping Trip

Thanks to space age technology, you can now obtain food, good tasting food, that requires only the addition of boiling water, a cover and a five-to-ten-minute simmer before serving. These freeze-dried foods, compressed space savers, have been to the moon and back with the astronauts. They have been used by the U.S. Polaris submarine fleet for several years. And, now they are ready for every camper to enjoy! They reduce original weight up to 90 percent, reduce original space needs by 75 percent to 90 percent and will store for many years if unopened. Their menu includes such main course entrees as vegetable beef stew, shrimp creole, rice and chicken, chili with beans, chicken stew, beef and rice with onions, and beef flavored rice. They also feature diced cooked beef, bacon bar, diced cooked chicken, green peas, green beans and corn. A brand, such as Mountain House, can be found in food stores, mountain shops, outdoor stores, sporting goods shops, back-packing shops, etc.

Regular lines of freeze-dried foods have held top popularity with back packers for several years. Entrees come packed in their own serving pouch or tray so there are no pots, pans or dishes to wash or carry. All you need is something to boil water in, a cup and a spoon. With the exception of the "compressed space savers," these freeze-dried foods are the lightest and most compact food you will find, and the most convenient. They come packaged in oxygen barrier foil envelopes or plastic polyethylene and will retain freshness for long periods of time. They are available in two-person meals and four-person meals. The number of entrees is endless: beef stew, shrimp creole, beef stroganoff, chicken stew, chili mac with beef, pre-cooked eggs with bacon, Mexican omelette, plus meats, vegetables, fruit, snacks, ice cream shakes, soups, beverages and desserts. These foods cost more than supermarket foods, but I think their light weight and cooking convenience justifies the extra cost.

Mosquitoes

Only the female mosquito bites, and when she shoves her beak into your skin, she is seeking the protein in your blood for her egg reproduction. Once she has fed, she can produce and lay eggs even if unfertilized. She will live about two weeks and lay over 200 eggs in a single mid-afternoon.

Indian Heaven has been called "Mosquito Heaven." The over 150 lakes and tarns contribute to a healthy mosquito population that remains active until the fall of the year. The mosquitoes come to life as the snow melts and remain until late August or the first of September.

Should you decide to visit this land in July or August, bring plenty of repellent. Be sure to keep the repellent well away from your eyes. I use the spray type, first spraying it into my hands, then rubbing it on my face.

If a mosquite finds an opening between your repellent applications, there is a way to minimize the itch. When the mosquito stuck her hollow stiletto into you, she first injected an anticoagulant to keep the blood thin so it would flow easily. If you will use the edge of your fingernail to sharply depress the center of the bite, making a "wheel spoke" pattern as you do so, you will disperse the anticoagulant and you will soon forget you were bitten.

Vitamin B_1 is said to act as a mosquito repellent. The Thiamine content in the vitamin is supposed to surface to the skin and discourage the mosquito's attack.

Compass

In the past a number of individuals have become lost in Indian Heaven. They have usually become disoriented in the high meadows on foggy or overcast days. Under capricious weather conditions the meadows, scattered groups of trees, the rolling terrain all tend to look alike when visibility becomes poor. This situation can be hazardous for the novice without a compass.

I experienced such a weather condition on a Trail 111 trip into Blue Lake in the fall of 1975. A heavy mist limited vision to less than 75 feet, and I suddenly realized that I had lost the trail. The situation would have been serious but for my knowledge of how to use a compass with a map.

Wandering away from a trail without a compass is a poor policy even though weather and visibility are good. The high country "look alike" terrain can be very deceptive and turn a delightful hiking experience into a nightmare.

A compass is only as good as your knowledge of its use. I recommend you obtain and read *Be Expert With Map and Compass* by Bjorn Kjellstrom, published by Charles Scribner's Sons.

If you are without a compass, your watch can help you find direction. Point the hour hand directly at the sun. Now, a line bisecting the arch between the hour hand and 12:00 o'clock will point south.

Traveling Alone

Do not travel alone! A badly sprained ankle or any number of acci-

106

dents or illnesses could leave you incapacitated without assistance from anyone. If you become lost, you have no one to communicate with for rescue. I recommend a minimum traveling party of three. In case of a serious accident or illness, one person can go for help while the other remains with the victim or a stretcher could be improvised to carry out the victim.

Falls

Falls are a common cause of injury to backpackers. A loaded pack can make your body topheavy and even on level ground, you can stumble and suffer injury. Hiking too close to your companion can also create trouble. A sudden stop by one hiker may lead to a collision. Keep a good distance between you and your companions and increase the distance on steep grades. Hiking downhill is more hazardous than hiking uphill because a slip can suddenly turn into a fall. On a steep downgrade take short steps and carefully watch your footing.

Backpackers suffer the most serious falls when they leave the trail. Climbing over logs, negotiating rock slides and crossing stream beds are particularly hazardous. Any off-trail hiking should be attempted with the utmost caution.

To Avoid Becoming Lost

1. Bring this book for trail map reference.
2. Have a compass and know how to use it.
3. Stay on the trail unless you are expert with map and compass.
4. Be observant as you travel. Watch the trail, remember your route, note landmarks such as mountains, streams, lakes and the lay of the land.
5. Never start a trip when weather conditions are bad or threatening.
6. Be sure and let someone know the route you are taking and when you plan to return. Inform them to notify the Skamania County Sheriff's office at Stevenson, Washington, or the Mt. Adams Ranger Station at Trout Lake, Washington, in the event you do not return as scheduled.
7. Be sure and check in when you do return.

What To Do If Lost

First, do not panic! Panic heads the list of killers of lost hikers and campers. Once they lose their power to reason they literally kill themselves. Sit down and take stock of your situation. Put fear out of your mind. How long have you been lost? How far have you strayed from the trail? Have your friends missed you and are they looking for you? Try three loud shouts or three shots from your gun. Your friends should answer with two of the above indicating they

have heard you.

If you receive no answers, you might back track following broken twigs, crushed grass or dislodged stones. Failing in this you should climb to a high point where you can rediscover landmarks. Should this fail you have two choices: (1) remain where you are and wait for rescue through the sound communications indicated above and by smoke signals from a small fire using green boughs, or (2) work your way back to civilization by walking the down slopes which will eventually lead to a water course which will lead to civilization.

Should you be caught out at night, the first rule is to stop walking. Build a fire on ground cleared to mineral soil and make yourself as comfortable as possible. Use your flashlight conservatively as you might need it later to attract rescuers. Three flashes indicate S.O.S. Keep in mind that exposure to the elements is more dangerous than hunger and thirst. You can live more than a week without food, and for three days without water, but only a few hours in severe weather. Stay near your fire. Improvise a "lean-to" shelter with poles and evergreen thatch.

Now, if you should find your way out to civilization, and your friends are still looking for you, get word immediately to a forest ranger, Skamania County Sheriff or some other responsible person who can stop the search. Failure to do so will make you mighty unpopular with your rescuers.

First Aid

Your first aid kit is useless unless you know how to use it.

Rather than get into all the subjects of how to treat burns, abrasions, broken bones, etc., we recommend you obtain and read the *American Red Cross First Aid Textbook* published by Doubleday and Company. It covers everything from mouth-to-mouth resuscitation to removal of fishhooks.

First aid kits are also available with enclosed instructions on how to treat various injuries.

Lightning

During the summer months thunderstorms do occur in Indian Heaven. They can be upon the hiker or camper in nearly an instant. They pass at about 30 miles per hour and usually only the front of the storm produces lightning. The best precautions to take are to avoid exposed ridges, large isolated trees, pinnacles, or other prominent points that attract lightning bolts. Keep a low profile by sitting or lying down.

Eunice Lake (opposite)

Other Common Hazards

Sharp instruments and fire are two common hazards campers must guard against. A knife or an axe must be treated with respect when used in camp chores such as cutting rope, shaving tinder, cleaning fish or splitting wood.

Hot pots and pans should be handled with aforethought. Boiling water, spilled on your foot, could put you out of action and a burned hand could make you miserable for the rest of the trip.

A knife can slip and gash a finger or palm all too easily. Even when used in necessary camp chores, such as cutting rope, shaving tinder for a fire, a knife must be treated with respect.

When handling sharp instruments or hot cooking equipment, keep in mind that professional medical attention is many miles away from Indian Heaven trails or campsites.

Note: some of the material included in the Health, Safety, Comfort and Survival section of this book was adapted from *The Complete Beginner's Guide To Backpacking* by Richard B. Lyttle. Copyright© 1975 by Richard B. Lyttle. Doubleday & Company, Inc., Publishers.

Hunting Season Danger

I avoid hiking and camping in Indian Heaven during the regular Washington State deer and elk hunting seasons. Although I have never met a hunter in the high country, I did run into a few on the lower section of Trail 171 in 1975 while on a hike into the race track. I was not wearing a bright hat or jacket like most hunters wear and it was a most uncomfortable experience. I finally resorted to giving periodic shouts just as I do to warn the bears when I am on a trail showing bear signs.

Altitude Sickness

At high altitudes air contains far less volume of oxygen than it does at sea level. In addition, the lack of air pressure limits the amount of available oxygen forced through the lung walls into the blood stream. The symptoms of altitude sickness are listlessness, loss of appetite, weakness, apathy, nausea, dizziness and drowsiness. The treatment is rest, a few deep breaths, nourishment from simple sugars like candy, and a return to lower elevations. This condition is unlikely to occur if you are in good physical condition, eat a well balanced diet, and take short preliminary hikes into high altitudes before attempting the long difficult ones.

110

Hyperventilation

This reaction to altitude is caused by too rapid breathing and decrease of the carbon dioxide level in the blood causing lightheadedness and cold feeling. The victim becomes apprehensive and excited. The treatment consists in calming the victim and having him relax and breathe into a glove, bag or hat until normal breathing is restored. The preventative is the same as for altitude sickness.

Hypothermia

Hypothermia is the rapid and progressive mental and physical collapse resulting from lowering the inner temperature of the human body. It is caused by exposure to cold, aggravated by wet, wind and exhaustion. Hypothermia can result in death if left untreated. The symptoms are fits of shivering, vague, slurred speech, memory lapses, fumbling hands, lurching walk, drowsiness, exhaustion and apparent unconcern about physical comfort. These symptoms are usually noticed by others before the victim is aware of them. The treatment consists in getting the victim out of the wind and wet, into dry clothes, and the restoring of body temperature with warm drinks, quick energy foods, body contact and a warm sleeping bag.

Many people mistakenly associate the occurrence of hypothermia with winter weather conditions of ice and snow. Hypothermia can actually develop at 50-degree air temperature if there is a cold wind factor accompanied by wetness. The prevention is to take suitable clothing for the worst expected weather and to avoid exhaustion.

Hypothermia is a critical problem and a victim should be given professional medical attention as soon as is possible.

U. S. Geological Survey Topographic Maps

U. S. Geological Survey topographic maps will tell you just about anything you want to know about the Indian Heaven back country. They give airplane views of the lakes (blue color), the forests (green), and once you learn to read their contour intervals you can approximate how much uphill and downhill hiking you will do on a given trip. They will help you determine landmarks such as mountains and other features to be used as reference points to keep you from getting lost. They are particularly helpful on off-trail hikes when oriented with a compass.

Four quadrangle maps are required to cover all of the Indian Heaven back country. They are "Lone Butte, Washington"; "Wind River, Washington"; "Sleeping Beauty, Washington," and "Willard, Washington." They are available at many mountaineering stores, or can be ordered from the U.S. Geological Survey, P.O. Box 25286, Federal

Center, Denver, Colorado 80225. They cost $1.25 each. Be sure and request a free copy of the booklet, *Topographic Maps*. This booklet contains many colored illustrations and much basic information about the maps and how to use them.

Do not depend on the accuracy of trail locations shown on a U.S. Geological Survey map, however, as the forest service may change a trail route after the map is issued.

Physical Conditioning

Physical adjustment and conditioning are an absolute prerequisite to tackling the Indian Heaven back country. The trails that lead to the high places are strenuous and the higher you climb the thinner the air becomes. The unconditioned, office-working, lowlander may seek the beauties of Indian Heaven, but end up in a heaven from which he will not return. Unless you are in top physical shape and already have some camping experience, you should definitely not begin with an overnight trip. You should take at least two moderate day trips prior to an extensive hiking and camping trip.

My physical conditioning starts at least three months before the hiking season. I first obtain a complete physical examination. If the doctor should detect a problem, there is still time for treatment prior to the first hike. Then I take long neighborhood walks, making sure to include uphill and downhill terrain.

When the magic day arrives I set up a base camp at one of the many forest service campgrounds near Indian Heaven. From this base camp I start my day-hike conditioning.

The first day I hike into Thomas Lake on Trail 111 and wander around the group of lakes in that area. The trail length is only ¾ mile, but by the time I have seen all the lakes I have hiked another half mile and a total of two miles when I return to the car. On this trip my pack is loaded with food and equipment for a day hike.

The second day I hike into Placid Lake and on to Chenamus Lake via the Placid Lake Trail 29 and Trail 29A. This hike represents a round trip distance of exactly three miles. For this trip I again load my pack with food and equipment for a day hike but add equipment for a combined hiking and camping trip. The reason for the added equipment is to become accustomed to the pack weight I will be carrying on the camping trip the following day.

By now I have hiked a total of five miles, exercised my muscles and lungs at elevations to 4,300 feet, experienced two nights of warm-up camping and feel confident to move into the Indian Heaven back country.

I have a simple rule about hiking. I never push myself to the point I cannot breathe comfortably and carry on a conversation.

Here are some hiking suggestions to make your trip more enjoyable: (They are excerpted from an article written by Steve Netherby, camping editor of *Field & Stream Magazine*, in that magazine's February, 1976 issue.)

(1) Breathe in rhythm with your steps. For instance, inhale every time your left boot strikes the trail. When the air is thinner, or the grade is steeper, you may inhale every time your left foot touches the slope, or as each foot hits, or twice as each foot hits. But keep a conscious rhythm. This will not only give you something to think about, it will help your heart hold a steady, comfortable beat.

(2) Inhale deeply, deeper as the work gets harder. Your body demands plenty of oxygen to perform hard labor. Deep-breathing helps speed the oxygen to where it is needed, including the muscles of your legs. Also, at higher altitudes you will need to inhale more deeply than at sea level to draw in the same amount of air. Anticipate your body's oxygen needs. Start your deep breathing early rather than waiting until you have built up an "oxygen debt." Another point to remember is that forced deep breathing while hiking can help ward off headache and other symptoms of altitude sickness.

(3) Exhale forcibly on those heavy upslopes through pursed lips. This expels more of the old air and makes way for more new air in your lungs. Deep inhaling and hard exhaling, you will sound like and hopefully feel like, a steam engine chugging up a steep slope.

(4) Keep a steady pace at all times, robotlike on the hard pulls. The hiker who spurts burns up energy and tires his muscles fast. It is the slow, steady climber who makes the high country first, with the most strength to spare. Even on level ground, learn to walk steadily with rhythm.

(5) Do the "rest step," sometimes called the mountaineer's lock step. Ascending a trail, plant the uphill foot, knee bent, and rest momentarily on the straightened downhill leg, knee locked. This way you are actually resting at each step and there is no weight on the uphill leg, since all the weight is being supported by the rigid bone structure of the downhill leg. Then push forward with the downhill foot and rock forward on a straightened uphill leg until the new uphill foot can be planted. The steeper the slope,

the shorter your steps should be. You should be aware of very little straining of the muscles of the upper leg. With practice, the rest step can be modified to suit almost any pace short of a jog and any slope gradient.

To ease the job of the calf muscles, rock through each step, where possible, with lug soles flat on the ground. Push off with the ball of the foot as lightly as you can.

When moving up a steep trail with an extra heavy pack on, try rocking your upper body forward from the waist as your upper leg swings forward.

So, breathe deeply, in rhythm with your steps. Walk with a steady pace and, using the rest step, conserve energy.

U. S. Forest Service Map Unreliable

The Indian Heaven portion of the 1976 Gifford Pinchot National Forest Recreation Map is sketchy, incomplete and contains many errors. Much of the newly constructed Pacific Crest National Scenic Trail No. 2000 is not shown at all and other trails are either non-existent, located in error, or not numbered. This is unfortunate because another map will not be published for several years. The previous map was issued in 1969. You can rely on the road and campground locations shown on the map, but not on the trail locations.

I cannot guarantee that the map shown in this book is one hundred percent correct, but it is much more reliable than the forest service map.

PART 4:

Trail Needs and Future Outlook for Indian Heaven

SHORT CUT TRAIL
NO. 171 A
↑ TRAIL 2000   1

RACE TRACK TRAIL
NO. 171
↑ CASCADE CREST TRAIL   ½
← ROAD N605   2
RED MT. LOOKOUT   1 →

INDIAN HEAVEN TRAIL NEEDS

In the face of ecological efforts and the work by environmentalists, the small allocation of monies for proper management of public recreation is grossly inadequate and is a reflection of priorities of those who administer funds. Gifford Pinchot would not have liked this.

In the fiscal year 1976 and the three month interim fiscal year, only $47,000 was allocated for the planning, condition surveys, signing, construction of new trails, and maintenance of 1,018 miles of existing trails in the Gifford Pinchot National Forest. Sixty-four thousand dollars was promised for the fiscal year ending September 30, 1977, an improvement over the previous year, but a drop in the bucket when one considers a cost of $8,000 to $25,000 to build one mile of new trail.

The result of this funding inadequacy has been the abandonment of many miles of existing trails and the deterioration of inventoried trails.

In Indian Heaven, only the Pacific Crest National Scenic Trail No. 2000 has received attention in recent years. The balance of inventoried trails are in various stages of neglect while other trails have been eliminated.

The Mt. Adams District Ranger commented on the condition of some of the trails and on the inadequacy of trail signing in reply to my letter requesting information: "We agree with your general comments. The key to proper management of the Indian Heaven area is funding for people and materials to accomplish the tasks you describe."

I wrote the Gifford Pinchot National Forest Trail Coordinator, inquiring why some Indian Heaven trails were being abandoned. My letter was answered by an "Education Specialist" who wrote:

"The elimination of trails in the Indian Heaven area was largely due to their undesirable location in regard to the resource damage they were causing. Having trails located through meadows has created serious problems with proper surface water drainage and the soil is not able to withstand the volume of traffic. **They also were unable to be maintained properly.**"

My observation of trails through meadows differs from theirs. Many

Opposite: Sign confusion near Indian Race Track.

of these trails are hard to follow. In the past, the Forest Service installed brightly painted posts to be followed as guides through the meadow to where the trail continued beyond the meadow. To be sure, I have observed some problems related to drainage, but these could be easily corrected.

Clay G. Beal and Mervin F. Wolf stated the problem and solution very clearly in their 1966 National Forest Recreation Plan for Indian Heaven:

"Trails will be located to minimize drainage problems across meadows, but should not attempt to avoid meadows. **Some of the most scenic vistas are observed where trails traverse meadows.** It is not necessary, however, that trails traverse the middle of meadows; **drainage problems may be avoided by skirting the higher ground at the edge of meadows.**"

In 1975, 1976 and 1977, the Pacific Crest National Scenic Trail No. 2000 was rerouted away from lakes and meadows in many parts of Indian Heaven. This change of policy prompted me to write another letter of inquiry to the Mt. Adams District Ranger. The following paragraph is taken from his reply:

"In most cases where there are trails directly to lakes, there is rather heavy overuse of them. We would like to avoid this happening. **We have felt it is better to let people seek them out.**"

His reply sounded reasonable until I gave it some afterthought and found I disagreed for the following reasons: (1) People are going to find the lakes and use them in any event; (2) Hikers may become injured while walking off the trail through rough terrain carrying a top-heavy pack (falls are the most common cause of hiker injury); and (3) A few individuals, unfamiliar with a compass, may become disoriented and lose their way.

Heaven knows it is the high lakes, meadows and wild flowers that are the major attractions in Indian Heaven. I consider it unfair to deprive the visitor of the convenient enjoyment of these attractions by routing trails away from them. The current problem could be solved if the Forest Service would construct short side trails into the lakes and meadows.

Hikers' boots are not the cause of Indian Heaven trail deterioration, but horses' hooves are. The result of the compression of horses' hooves is particularly noticeable on forest slopes where melting snow and rain flow down the trail rut to eventually create troughs — in some places, knee deep, far worse than any trail condition you might see in the meadows.

118

Ban horses from the trails until the first of September is one solution. This would give the soil a chance to dry out and become more impervious to wear and tear.

A new section of the Pacific Crest National Scenic Trail between Junction Lake and Blue Lake was completed in 1975. It was built, north to south, around the west side of East Crater, part way up the mountain, to replace the old abandoned trail in the meadow below. Horses walked the trail right after the 1976 snow melt. I have never before seen a new trail change from a thing of beauty to a pigpen in less than three weeks.

Trail riding is fun and I enjoy it immensely, but I will never ride a horse on an Indian Heaven trail until the fall season is well under way.

Here are a few trail developments that the Forest Service should accomplish in order to provide for the adequate disbursement of people throughout the area and to meet the needs of the growing public for a recreation experience:

1. Reconstruct and bring up to standard all trails within the area. This would include all previously abandoned trails. Some relocation would be required along the same general location or route. Meadow trails, for example, could be relocated skirting the higher ground at the edge of the meadow.
2. Relocate and construct the Placid Lake Trail No. 29 (old Lone Butte Trail) between Placid Lake and the Pacific Crest National Scenic Trail No. 2000 via Wood Lake. This change would improve access to Wood Lake from the west and eliminate that portion of the present trail with excessive grade.
3. Construct a short trail from the Pacific Crest National Scenic Trail No. 2000 up over the rim and down into the bowl of East Crater.
4. Complete construction of the Gifford Peak (Way) Trail between the Darlene Lakes and the Pacific Crest National Scenic Trail No. 2000. This easterly extension would provide another much needed loop trail via the Indian Race Track Trails No. 171A and No. 171.
5. Construct a new trail commencing on Trail No. 34 at a point northeast of Lemei Rock and proceeding south around the east face of Lemei Rock, thence southwest along a number of lakes and connecting to the East Crater Trail No. 48. This would provide another needed loop trail.
6. Construct short side trails from the Pacific Crest National Scenic Trail to Deer Lake, Clear Lake, Lake Toke-Tie and the huge meadows lying to the west of the trail between Acker and Junction lakes. The use of these trails and lakes would not be as heavy as the Forest Service would like to believe, because the through

traffic on the Crest Trail would bypass a lot of them due to time schedules.

7. Construct short side trails into Brader Lake and the largest of the Umtux lakes from Trail No. 111.

The Forest Service might be encouraged to take a stronger look at our recreation needs if we, the traveler, conducted ourselves in a more considerate manner. Here are a few "Good Conduct" rules:

(1) Do not smoke while traveling.
(2) Do not shortcut trails.
(3) Do not deface or knock down trail signs.
(4) Do not steal trail signs.
(5) Do not drop paper wrappers, cans, bottles or anything else on or alongside the trail.
(6) Do not camp right alongside a trail.
(7) Do not deposit body waste near a trail.

Many Forest Service people learn to dislike recreationists because of the problems they cause. You can help turn this attitude around by practicing good conduct while on the trail and in the camp.

INDIAN HEAVEN'S FUTURE

Indian Heaven has no lasting protection against logging. At this writing (in 1977) a timber sale sign is posted at the very trail head of Trail 29 within 2,500 feet of Placid Lake. Another sale sign is posted at the trail head of Trail 111 within 3,000 feet of Thomas, Dee, Heather, Eunice and Kwad-dis lakes.

In recent years, extensive clear-cuts have been made in the northwest section of Indian Heaven. These clear-cuts eliminated approximately two miles of Trail 27, which then extended from Placid Lake to the Sawtooth huckleberry fields. The clear-cuts, additionally, encroached to within 2,500 feet of Wood Lake near Bird Mountain.

The western section of Indian Heaven has fared no better. A number of clear-cuts have been made along Road N605, one of which encroaches within 2,500 feet of Thomas and Kwad-dis lakes.

The southern and eastern sections have seen drastic intrusions of logging roads extending into Indian Heaven like the arms of an octopus. The chain saw has chewed to the very shores of Lake Comcomly (named after the Indian chief) and some of the Forlorn Lakes.

Forest Service timber sale plans do not bode well for the future of Indian Heaven. An "Action Plan" projecting resource development proposals for the years 1977 through 1981 contain the following planned sales: (1) 2.7 million board feet of timber from 310 acres would be offered for sale south of Road 123 near the Smoky Creek Campground, involving 1.6 miles of new road construction.

The result of this operation would be the elimination of Trail 34 between Road 123 and the intersection with Trail 102 and the diversion of the Trail 34 trail head to Little Goose Campground.

(2) The sale of 6.3 million board feet of timber from 158 acres of clear-cuts northwest of Road N627. New road construction would involve 2.1 miles. The result of this operation would be the obliteration of approximately one-half mile of the East Crater Trail No. 48.

The "Action Plan" includes an editorial statement which gives me additional concern. "Certain sales are planned within the boundaries of some of the identified roadless areas." (Indian Heaven falls in this classification.)

The "Action Plan" has 93 pages, but only one page is devoted to recreation. The opening statement reads, **"Recreation financing continues to be limited."** This statement pretty well sums up what has happened to the Forest Service insofar as public recreation is concerned.

It appears that the major concern of the U.S. Forest Service is the production and marketing of timber, so much so that everything revolves around timber management. Here are the words of a retired Forest Service employee who spent 22 years in the service:

"If one has aspirations to eventually become a U.S. Forest Supervisor, he must plan to advance through the ranks of timber management. Somewhere along the line he may work with some other branch for a short time, but no other branch offers him a chance to build himself a small empire in the district or become a staff member in the supervisor's office. **Timber is adequately funded while other branches are not.** The Forest Service is pressured from Washington, D.C. This pressure is first exerted on the Regional Office and in turn to the Regional Forester and then down through the District. The ever present message is, 'The economy of the country depends upon timber.' "

I will be the first to agree that the economy of the country has some dependence on timber, but I have reservations about the practicability of harvesting timber at high elevations, and for these reasons:

(1) It takes up to 300 years for a tree to grow to maturity. Even

then, the tree is diminutive in size compared to the fast growing Douglas fir at lower elevations.

(2) The successful replanting of trees in clear-cuts is doubtful. The much publicized "sustained yield" may turn out to be a one time harvest.

(3) The watershed will suffer damage that mother nature would not be able to correct for several centuries.

Regardless of the merits or demerits of the above arguments, I do take a firm stand against logging high areas with unquestionable scenic beauty and with high recreational values. There is no place for the chain saw in Indian Heaven. Sigurd F. Olson, internationally known author-conservationist, expressed my feelings exactly, when he said,

"If our population keeps exploding, if our industrial land base keeps expanding, if we keep adding another million square miles of blacktop to the surface of the earth, the most unique thing a piece of country can have will be its naturalness. To see a place as beautiful as God made it — that will be unique in time to come."

Indian Heaven is one of those places Sigurd F. Olson talks about, and I am vitally concerned about its future.

In the late 60's, two Forest Service studies were made of Indian Heaven. The first was called **National Forest Recreation Area** Gifford Pinchot National Forest **Indian Heaven Unusual Interest Area** (back country). It was prepared by Clay G. Beal, dated February 17, 1966, signed by Mervin F. Wolf on November 12, 1968, and **Recommended for Approval** by Ross Williams on March 26, 1969.

The second study was called **Indian Heaven Roadless Area Multiple Use Survey**, an analysis of the inter-relationship of the proposed **Indian Heaven Roadless Area**. It was prepared by Paul L. Read and Mervin F. Wolf and signed by both on December 17, 1969, and **Recommended for Approval** by Ross Williams on December 19, 1969.

Both studies acknowledged the Forest Service has long recognized the beauty and recreational value of Indian Heaven. (The first recreation plan was prepared in 1936.) They agreed that no timber should be cut in the area except for the control and salvage of extraordinary insect disease, wind throw or fire loss. They recommended that existing trails be maintained or relocated to eliminate excessive grades and that new ones be built, particularly noting a need for loop trails. They emphasized that the Indian Heaven area was needed to meet the need for wilderness-type recreation on the Gifford Pinchot National Forest. They further recommended that boundaries be

Opposite: Clear cutting within 2500 feet of Placid Lake.

established and delineated on the ground.

Neither of these proposals was approved. Responsible Forest Service people have stated, "We doubt the proposals were given serious consideration because to establish boundaries would eliminate future timber harvest within those boundaries." One was heard to say, "If even a small portion of the present Indian Heaven survives, you won't have any trouble determining its boundaries because they will be well established by clear-cuts."

It is difficult to understand that the U.S. Forest Service would reject either of these proposals on the basis of timber management considerations, since the projected boundaries consisted of only 15,600 acres of the highest country containing mostly non-merchantable timber.

In any event, the projected boundaries encompassed too small an area and would allow logging on all the approach slopes including most trail approaches up to and around a number of lakes.

Indian Heaven boundaries should include an area much larger than the proposals made by Clay G. Beal, Mervin F. Wolf and Paul L. Read.

I recommend that boundaries be established to include all of that land inside perimeter roads described as follows: Commencing at the northerly junction of Forest Service Road N605 with N73; thence N.E. on N73 to 123; thence S.E. on 123 to N604; thence S.W. on N604 to N627; thence S.W. on N627 to N638; thence S. to N60; thence S.W. on N60 to N605; thence N. on N605 to the point of beginning. The Surprise Lakes should also be included.

I am convinced that the only way to save Indian Heaven is to have it established as a wilderness area. If this is not accomplished, the same pattern of clear-cut encroachment will continue until there's little or nothing left of the area.

To obtain a wilderness designation is not going to be easy. The timber industry puts unrelenting pressure on the Forest Service. Their powerful industry trade associations are lobbying constantly for logging rights to more timber. They demand increases of harvest levels, more roads and the modifying of existing regulations. They put constant pressure on the Forest Service through Congress or the Administration.

I am sure the general public would be upset if they were aware of the extent to which the timber industry influences the Forest Service nd of the extent to which public recreation suffers as a consequence. Things have gotten completely out of balance. The Multiple Use Act, Public Law 86-517, 86th Congress, June 12, 1960, states: 'It is the policy of the Congress that the National Forests are established and shall be administered for **outdoor recreation**, range, timber, watershed, and wildlife and fish purposes."

It states further:

'Due consideration shall be given to the relative values of the various resources in particular areas — **areas of wilderness** which are consistent with the purposes and provisions of the Act."

There can be no question that Indian Heaven qualifies for wilderness consideration under the terms of the act.

I am heartened and encouraged by the July, 1976, creation of a 393,000 acre Alpine Lakes wilderness area in Washington's Central Cascades. Years of intermittent feuding over the proposal culminated in months of intense negotiations in 1975 involving environmentalists, recreation groups and the ever-present timber industry. The legislation was opposed by the Forest Service who sided with the timber interests. The creation of this new wilderness proves what can be accomplished when a concerned and determined effort is made.

I strongly urge you to visit Indian Heaven, view its beauty, and then write your Representative and Senator urging them to set aside this wondrous land of lakes, craters, meadows and mountains as a wilderness area.

If you cannot visit Indian Heaven, write anyway, or join an organization such as "The Mountaineers" or "Wilderness Society" who work to preserve areas such as this.

For as long as can be remembered, Indian Heaven was the beloved summer home of the Northwest Indians. Much of the land, though threatened, remains as it was then. If we can manage to create an Indian Heaven Wilderness Area, we will preserve this paradise, not only for our enjoyment, but for the enjoyment of future generations — "To see a place that is still untouched, which is still as beautiful as God made it."

BIBLIOGRAPHY

Books

Attwell, Jim, *Columbia River Gorge History* (Volume One), Tahlki Books, 1974

Attwell, Jim, *Columbia River Gorge History* (Volume Two), Tahlki Books, 1975

Place, Marion T., *On The Trail of Bigfoot*, Dodd, Mead and Com pany, 1974

Thomas, Edward Harper, *Chinook, A History and Dictionary*, Bin fords and Mort, Publishers, 1975

Horn, Elizabeth, *Wild Flowers I The Cascades*, Touchstone Press 1972

Lyttle, Richard B., *The Complete Beginner's Guide to Backpacking* Doubleday and Company, Inc., 1975

Booklets

U. S. Forest Service, *Indian Heaven Unusual Interest Area, Multiple Use Survey*, 1966

U. S. Forest Service, *Indian Heaven Roadless Area, Multiple Use Survey*, 1969

Magazines

Eaton, Randall, *Puma-Mystery Cat*, Pacific Search, 1975

Netherby, Steve, *Excerpts from Articles by the Camping Editor* Field and Stream

Brochure

U. S. Department of Agriculture, *Winter Travel in the Nationa Forests*

APPENDIX

SKAMANIA COUNTY "BIG FOOT"
ORDINANCE NO. 69-01

BE IT HEREBY ORDAINED BY THE BOARD OF COUNTY COMMISSIONERS OF SKAMANIA COUNTY:

WHEREAS, there is evidence to indicate the possible existence in Skamania County of a nocturnal primate mammal variously described as an ape-like creature or a sub-species of Homo Sapian; and

WHEREAS, both legend and purported recent sightings and spoor support this possibility, and

WHEREAS, this creature is generally and commonly known as a "Sasquatch," "Yeti," "Bigfoot," or "Giant Hairy Ape," and

WHEREAS, publicity attendant upon such real or imagined sightings has resulted in an influx of scientific investigators as well as casual hunters, many armed with lethal weapons, and

WHEREAS, the absence of specific laws covering the taking of specimens encourages laxity in the use of firearms and other deadly devices and poses a clear and present threat to the safety and well-being of persons living or traveling within the boundaries of Skamania County as well as to the creatures themselves,

THEREFORE BE IT RESOLVED that any premeditated, willful and wanton slaying of any such creature shall be deemed a felony punishable by a fine not to exceed Ten Thousand Dollars ($10,000.00) and/or imprisonment in the county jail for a period not to exceed Five (5) years.

BE IT FURTHER RESOLVED that the situation existing constitutes an emergency and as such this ordinance is effective immediately.

ADOPTED this 1st day of April, 1969.

BOARD OF COMMISSIONERS OF SKAMANIA COUNTY

By _____
Chairman

APPROVED:

_____
Skamania County Prosecuting Attorney

ABOUT THE AUTHOR

Mel Hansen is a successful real estate broker with offices in Portland, Oregon. He says:

"I discovered the Indian Heaven back country, quite by chance, while wandering the Cascade Mountains in southwest Washington. I fell in love with the country, but couldn't make up my mind whether to keep it to myself or to share it with others. The decision was made three years later when it became apparent that the encroaching chain saw would eventually destroy Indian Heaven unless it was publicized and people rallied to protect it."